The Hero of Jersey Street

by

Bob Murphy

The Conrad Press

The Hero of Jersey Street

Published by The Conrad Press in the United Kingdom 2024

Tel: +44(0)1227 472 874
www.theconradpress.com
info@theconradpress.com

ISBN 978-1-915494-99-3

Copyright ©Robert Donald Murphy 2024

All rights reserved.

Typesetting and Cover Design by: Levellers.
'Wanted poster 'design by Shayla Durbois.

Illustrations by Shayla Durbois

The Conrad Press logo was designed by Maria Priestley.

Printed and bound in Great Britain by Clays Ltd, Elcograf S.p.A.

The Hero of Jersey Street

Chapter One

The Big Bang

I was only ten years old when the big bang occurred in my life. I remember it like it was yesterday. The big bang I'm talking about was my 5th grade field trip to Fenway Park in Boston to watch the Red Sox play baseball. That was my first experience seeing a Major League Baseball game. The date was June 8, 1950, and at that time nothing mattered more to me than the Red Sox and I do mean nothing! However, this isn't a baseball story, it's a story about how one game influenced my life. It was a surprise to me because I never dreamed that a baseball game would leave a video memory imprinted on my brain, but I've always been thankful for it. Here's how the whole thing happened.

After living for three years in the graceful town of Milton, about a dairy farm Southwest of Boston, my family relocated to the Chicago area for the following four years. We first lived in Niles, then Park Ridge, both towns about fifteen miles Northwest of the city. It was 1946 when we moved back east to the Boston suburb of Quincy, and it was there that I fell in love with baseball. I read that Branch Rickey, the owner of the Brooklyn Dodgers, said, 'Baseball is a game of inches.' He was right and that made it exciting to me. It also seemed to be true of my life – it frequently seemed like a game of inches, making it exciting, to me anyway. My mother, though, had a different opinion. She often thought my behavior was troubling and unacceptable. I'll explain more about that shortly if you'll bear with me for a while.

Now, seventy-three years after that 1950 game, when some people my age might be grasping at wispy, fading memories, my recollection seems to be clear and lucid enough. To quantify that, I'd estimate the information I'm about to share to be at least eighty percent bona fide in spite of the time that has elapsed. Any distortions that have crept in over the years should be thought of as a few dashes of literary salt, a pinch or two of literary pepper, and in a couple of cases, an effort to protect the innocent. Nonetheless, you can't bet the farm on the story because it isn't a documentary, it's a kid's story and we all know what that can mean.

At the time of the big bang, my family was living in the Wollaston Beach section of Quincy, a shoreline city with a population of about 75,000 people. There were six of us, my parents – Jim and Adelaide Murphy, two older sisters – Dorothy and Barbara, an older brother, Jimmy, and me, 'the baby' of the family. I was known as Bobby to my family and Murph to my friends. I hated being called Bobby. My mother hated me being called Murph. That was only the tip of the iceberg of differences that separated us.

My siblings ranged in age from nine to thirteen years older than me; my parents were thirty-seven years older. Needless to say, there was a wide gap in communication between them and me, especially my parents and me, more especially my mother and me. It seemed like the only things we had in common were our last name and the house where we lived.

I was two months shy of seven when we moved east. By then, we had relocated from one state to another, one town to another, one neighborhood to another, one church to another, and one school to another enough times that I felt like I was part of a family of nomads.

One of the schools – Saint Paul of the Cross – was in Park Ridge. It was run by an order of nuns called The Catholic Sisters of Mercy who acted more like a military police unit than schoolteachers. Believe me, the nuns I met never showed me any mercy. Before going there, I was warned by my siblings that nuns were ornery people. Apparently, Dorothy, Jimmy and Barbara had all attended parochial schools before we moved to the Chicago area. My brother Jimmy said that nuns wore long, black capes called habits because some of them were in the habit of carrying concealed weapons, such as guns, knives and brass knuckles. I was already terrified of nuns before I ever met one of them.

Dealing with parents, siblings, new friends, new neighbors, new classmates, new schools, new teachers and, most of all, the Sisters of Mercy, was risky, life-threatening business for me. Just the experiences with the nuns were enough to permanently warp my mind. Some days I felt like I was going over Niagara Falls in a wooden barrel, which at the time was a terrifying, daredevil publicity stunt that usually ended in tragedy or death.

My mother was capable of inventing city, state and federal laws to control my behavior. The issues usually had something to do with what was convenient for her, and sometimes my father, too. What I wanted and what my brother and two sisters wanted didn't seem to be nearly as important. Eventually, I learned it was more efficient to go ahead and do things without asking for permission, even if there might be consequences later.

My parents were 100 percent Irish-Catholic, which was a double-edged sword, sometimes a benefit because of the sense of order it provided and at other times a hindrance, mostly because of the scrupulosity it required. If you're not familiar with anything similar, my parents' world was like a radical version of Roman Catholicism, a holdover from the Holy Crusades and the Spanish Inquisition. The Catholic Church had ten commandments; my family had thirteen. The additional three were: '(#11) Children should be seen and not heard; (#12) You're damned if you do and damned if you don't; (#13) No matter what you think, you're wrong.' Plus, of course, there was the infamous 'Murphy's Law' which proposed that 'Anything that can go wrong will go wrong, and at the worst possible moment.' My mother was seriously controlling, my father was seriously intimidating, my siblings were seriously disturbing, and the Sisters of Mercy were seriously oppressive. It was a lot for me to deal with. To survive, I had to become resilient and optimistic.

Milton, Niles and Park Ridge were small towns

while Quincy, although much larger, had a small-town atmosphere because the neighborhoods seemed like separate villages. More suburban than urban, Quincy had a large mix of blue-collar workers due in no small part to 10,000 or so employees at its Fore River Shipyard. The city also had a municipal hospital, a U.S. Naval air station, a private college campus, two public high schools, two draw bridges, two private golf courses, public transportation including train service and blocks of retail shops including three department stores. Nobody had heard of shopping malls back then so residents from surrounding towns, mostly people not wanting to travel to Boston, considered Quincy to be the shopping Mecca for Boston's South Shore communities.

Some neighborhoods were more like foreign countries, composed of different nationalities and religions. Ours was named the Beechwood Knoll and the people there seemed to be more Irish-Catholics than other nationalities and religions. My mother seemed to feel comfortable about that. I never thought that my father cared who or what our neighbors were, as long as they didn't ask to borrow his tools.

That's how it was when we moved there. My mother used to say there was a better class of people where we lived to which my father replied, 'You're nuts if that's what you think. I'm Irish too but some of the worst people I know are your relatives.' But some of our neighbors were just as prejudiced as my mother. And that wasn't just in our neighborhood. Some of the kids at my school who lived in other neighborhoods talked about what their families said about Irish-Catholics. People's identities went all the way to totally unimportant issues like what brand of milk they drank and the kind of bread they ate. I had no idea why that was important; it just was.

The decade from 1946, when my family moved to Quincy, through 1955, when rock 'n roll became wildly popular, was an amazing period, at least what I remember about it. 1946 was the year that the Red Sox won the American League pennant, although they lost the World Series. 1948 was the year that the Boston Braves won the National League pennant, although they lost the World Series. 1950 was the year that I attended my first Red Sox game with Miss DiMascio's 5th grade class, which was a life changing event, unlike anything else.

One of the things everyone in our family shared was patriotism. We were not just Irish-Catholics but also Irish Americans. I suppose that made us Irish-Catholic Americans and, as my parents insisted, we were 'damn proud of it.' Americans, as a whole, were post-war passionate about being Americans and, around Boston, patriotic feelings were running high.

American soldiers had successfully stormed Normandy Beach on the French side of the English Channel in 1944 where they helped to vanquish a German army, leading to the end of the war in Europe. The following year, U.S. Marines won a mountaintop victory on the South Pacific Island of Iwo Jima which was the turning point of the war effort against Japan. That was five months prior to the U.S. dropping atomic bombs on the Japanese mainland to end the insanity of Japanese pilots flying Kamikaze suicide missions against American ships.

Newspapers and radio broadcasts kept Americans aware of WWII on a daily basis, fuelling the patriotic spirit. My parents regularly listened in to a radio program by a news reporter named Walter Winchell, who started his broadcasts with the words, 'Good evening, Mr. and Mrs. America from border to border and coast to coast and all the ships at sea,' while the clicking sound of a telegraph key could be heard in the background. It wasn't high tech by today's standards, but it captured people's attention.

Chapter Two

Dazzling doodads

In case you missed the aftermath to WWII, the American economy was thriving. Jobs were plentiful, the minimum wage was seventy-five cents an hour, banks had money to lend, housing starts were exploding, and Baby Boomers were popping out from hospital maternity wards like kernels of Jiffy Pop from a stovetop frying pan. American cars evolved from function to form, angular to aerodynamic and plain to stylish. New car offerings from Detroit displayed dazzling doodads and chrome-coated curly-cues, including Pontiac's Indianhead hood ornaments with glowing amber-bright lights.

Most new American cars offered comfort options such as AM radios, thermostatic heaters and automatic transmissions. Safety features like power steering, power brakes, turn signals and side view mirrors were available. Foreign cars had barely dented the American car market regardless of what features they offered.

The price of a gallon of regular gasoline was slightly shy of twenty cents; a half dollar could buy enough gas to get a family around town for a weekend although typical auto mileage was only 15 miles per gallon. At that time, we didn't think that life could get much better. Little did we know that the automobile was about to dramatically change American society. Nearly every suburban family owned a car by then, some owned two and suburban women were applying for driver's licenses more often than wedding licenses. Typical middle-class families, like our clan, had a house, a car, a TV and four kids.

If your family had a new car, you were living the American dream and my family was doing exactly that. My father bought a new, black Buick Roadmaster in 1946 and exchanged it for another new, black Buick Roadmaster in 1950. In 1949, he took a giant leap in technology – he bought an RCA television set with a sixteen-inch picture tube. The Murphy family was moving on up to the big time in black and white!

At home, state of the art meant your dishes could be washed in an automated, gushing gadget instead of a porcelain, double sink and the newfangled TV in your living room would soon be connected to an outdoor antenna, up on the roof, replacing the indoor, V-shape rabbit ears that came with your set. Believe it or not, before outdoor antennas, some folks wrapped aluminium foil around the rabbit ears to improve reception. In those days, television was far from an exact science. In our neighborhood, families gathered nightly to watch tiny TV screens with colorless, sometimes snowy, sometimes wavy images that were transmitted from Boston's two TV stations. Nobody had heard of a remote control; people walked to the set when they wanted to change channels.

In the sky, commercial airliners were transitioning from propellers to jets. On the ground, the countryside was being criss-crossed by new, wide superhighways and toll booths were springing-up from coast to coast like dandelions following a spring rain. Whoever thought city buildings would be replaced by parking lots? Whoever thought highway motels with blinking neon signs would multiply like rabbits? Americans were on the move, life was speeding up and by 1950 most suburban families owned a car, some had two.

Meals were also speeding up, with fresh farm foods being replaced by quick-frozen TV dinners. Local, eat-in diners were being replaced by national, drive thru, fast food sites. Large communities had California-style drive-in restaurants with waitresses called car hops on roller skates bringing food to customers seated in their cars. Locally, we hadn't seen any McDonald's drive-thru restaurants yet, but by 1948 plans were on the drawing board for McDonald's franchises with serving windows, golden arches, billions of greasy fries and fifteen-cent burgers to begin spreading like a flu epidemic from San Diego to New York City.

Drive-in restaurants and drive-in movie theatres became favorite spots for teenage boys in hot rod cars to bring their dates for a little hoochie-coochie. Howard Johnson restaurants with orange roofs, orange steeples and twenty-eight flavors of ice cream including orange sherbet were opening at locations from beaches to interstate highways. The post-war era was an explosion of changing social styles, expanded travel, revolutionary eating habits, indestructible plastic toys, electric colors and home entertainment, mostly TV programs and sporting events. There were no such things as personal computers, laptops, iPads, GPS, email and text messaging. Away from your house, you had to locate a telephone booth and drop a coin into a slot to make a three-minute phone call. Obviously, at home or not, there was no need for anything called Wi-Fi.

Stand-up phone booths built with wooden frames, glass panels and bi-fold doors were used indoors and were about the size of upright coffins. They could be found in drug stores, five and dime stores, restaurants and the like. Others made with aluminium frames were used outdoors at street corners, bus terminals and train stations.

If you needed research information, there was no Google or Wikipedia. You went to the local library or referred to a set of home encyclopedias. The closest things to the Internet were Western Union Telegraph and the U.S. Post Office. Browsing meant scanning the latest magazines and newspapers at a news stand. As a nation, we hadn't been introduced to instant gratification yet; patience was still considered to be a virtue.

Magazine subscriptions, encyclopedias and vacuum cleaners were sold door to door. Local merchants offered trading stamps to customers and some people only shopped where trading stamps were used. I can remember my mother licking S&H green stamps and pasting them into redemption booklets at the table in our yellow and green kitchen. She'd study the catalogue to determine how many completed booklets she needed for that General Electric blender or whatever else she'd had her eye on.

At our house, my mother was responsible for school issues, meals, housekeeping, laundry, ironing, grocery shopping, banking and paying the bills. My father examined her check book periodically to be certain that she was using her $35 weekly budget wisely. In her mind, top of the round steak was good enough anytime it was on sale; mine too! And, Monday night was always 'leftovers' night, take it or leave it. The motto in our house was a penny saved is a penny earned. Families didn't use credit cards, we lived within our means. If all of those habits sound restrained, it was less stressful than today because most people didn't buy things until they could afford them. As a result, people seemed to be happier, and we were more satisfied with what we had.

Songs were mostly romantic until the 1950s – it was the Big Band Era. In 1950, Frank Sinatra was thirty-five years old and annual sales of his records topped a million copies. Elvis Presley was fifteen and hadn't cut a record yet but that would soon change. The sun was setting on the Big Bands, the street corner harmonies of Doo-Wop were in the air and who knew what digital music was? Every time I got my hands on eighty-nine cents, I'd be off to Jason's Music Shop in Quincy Center to buy the latest, top-selling forty-five RPM vinyl disc.

Life was good, life was simple, and most viewpoints were politically correct... but not all. If things weren't black, they were white. Gay meant cheerful. A tweet was a bird sound. Surfing was a West Coast beach sport. Nobody needed to learn how to operate digital apps with screwy names like Facebook, FaceTime, Twitter, Skype, Snapchat, Instagram, Spotify, TikTok and more. We didn't know what an algorithm was, much less how to spell or pronounce it. Electronic games were unheard of, other than pinball arcade games and most kids played outdoors year-round instead of in their bedrooms.

Unfortunately, segregation was the norm, especially in the Deep South. African Americans were known as colored people and even the NAACP used the term as exemplified by the last two initials in its name. Racial equality was moving at a snail's pace in spite of the flash-dancing Nicholas Brothers, songstress Ella Fitzgerald, trumpeter Louis Armstrong, bandleader Duke Ellington, the hugely popular Amos 'n Andy Show and baseball's #42, Jackie Robinson of the Brooklyn Dodgers. Gender equality was stuck in the mud of male supremacy, but the majority of people didn't recognize the social injustice of it. The reality was that most Americans didn't know much about political correctness at the time.

Grown men wore felt dress hats called fedoras, bow ties that actually needed to be tied, suspenders to hold up their slacks and garters to hold up their stockings. Women wore hats practically everywhere, white gloves to many activities and they couldn't enter a Catholic Church without some kind of covering on their heads. Women who needed to, squeezed into corsets and girdles with garters to hold up their nylon stockings. Even at ball games, crowds were dressed more like people who were going to church than going to a sporting event.

When I was a kid, women wore skirts that ended somewhere below their knees and shorts that ended just above their knees. It was the 3M code – modesty, moderation and morality were the principal ingredients. Women who varied from it were called 'brazen hussies' by my mother. What's more, if you were a Catholic, you had to recite the Catholic Code of Decency during Mass every so often, refusing to watch or listen to any risqué entertainment. To do otherwise was a mortal sin and would require a trip to Confession. Nevertheless, as long as the Roman Catholic Church didn't make baseball a sin, I was okay with being a Catholic.

Chapter Three

City of Presidents

Quincy was called the City of Presidents because it was home to the former houses of John Adams and John Quincy Adams, the second and sixth U.S. Presidents. Quincy was also famous for having been the home of John Hancock, the first signer of the Declaration of Independence, and his wife, Dorothy Quincy. It was there that the Fore River Shipyard built naval war ships and tankers and the Squantum Naval Air Station trained Navy pilots. WWII ended in 1945, the field trip to Fenway occurred five years later and news reports suggested we might soon be entering another war, this one in Korea.

Hancock Street, the main drag, still had streetcar tracks with overhead electrical cables. Quincy was connected to Boston by the Neponset River drawbridge, a metal span sometimes called 'thunder bridge' for its loud, baritone rumbling as rubber tires crossed the sections of its steel grid. Compared to other places where I'd lived, Quincy was the most interesting; there were endless things to see and do!

June 8, 1950, the day of our field trip, was a Thursday that could have won an award as being the most exciting day of my life. You can't possibly imagine how thrilling it was unless you were alive seventy-three years ago and realized how rarely those kinds of exceptional, exciting, entertaining events happened to a ten-year-old like me. The only entertainment at our house was my sister Barbara's record player, my table model radio, an assortment of board games like Parcheesi and Checkers, a deck of playing cards, and the sixteen-inch black and white TV in our living room. But the women at Rita's Hair Salon had convinced my mother that watching baseball on TV could ruin my eyesight, so keeping up with the Red Sox for me was restricted to radio play-by-play, TV newscasts and the sports section of The Boston Globe. The most annoying thing about my mother was her insistence that her parental decisions were absolute, without exception. The most annoying thing about my father was that he enforced her parental decisions, absolutely, without exception.

On the morning of the field trip to Fenway Park, sunbeams, like the glow from a thousand spotlights, broke through the colonial window three feet away from my bedroom pillow. According to my father, that kind of window was called 'double-hung,' but I never heard why. That was the window above the awninged porch on top of our garage, one of the windows that faced east toward Quincy Bay. As soon as my eyelids popped open, my brain's bugle started blowing those imaginary, doot-doot-datta-doot, doot-doot-datta-doot reveille sounds. I was so excited you'd have thought Santa Claus was bringing me that red Raleigh racing bike with the narrow tires, hand brakes and three-speed shifter, the bike I'd been dreaming about ever since I started dreaming.

Before my feet ever hit the floor, I had already envisioned myself on the Raleigh, whizzing through the streets of Quincy, pedalling along Chickatawbut Road where it snakes through the evergreen embankments of the Blue Hills Reservation, uphill past Houghton's Pond, heading west toward Milton. And there I am, hunched over the handlebars, hunkered down against a whistling wind whipping at my face, while moving at the speed of an Olympic athlete, pretending to be a caped crusader, taking in the colorful, fragrance of intimate green pine needles interwoven to form a colossal canopy above the slate blue outcroppings of granite boulders and ledges left behind by an ancient glacier 12,000 years earlier.

But I knew that neither Santa nor his sleigh would be coming in June to deliver presents; any kid with half a brain knew that. And, according to my father, that was exactly what I had – 'half a brain.' Between you and me, I wasn't as dumb as the rest of the family seemed to think but my father nevertheless liked to tell me in his deep, resonant voice, 'You're just a damned dope.'

Because it wasn't Christmas, I didn't expect there would be any Raleigh racing bike, but I was expecting the day to still become the most exciting day of my life. I could feel it in my bones, like whenever Don Kent, the WBZ-TV weatherman, forecasted rain long before the storm clouds rolled in. My mother used to say she could feel the rain coming in her bones, a day ahead of time because of her arthritis.

Once inside our black and white, subway-tiled, upstairs bathroom, a glob of Pepsodent toothpaste erased the overnight yellow from my smile. A splash of cold tap water made my cheeks faintly rosy and a dab of golden Brylcreem put my cowlick back where it belonged. I liked Brylcreem's bouncy radio jingle, especially the last line that went, 'Brylcreem – the girls will all pursue ya, they love to get their fingers in your hair.' What I didn't like so much was the greasy look it could leave on my head, so I only used enough to dab that infernal cowlick of mine.

I grabbed fresh underwear from my chest-of-drawers, buttoned up the white short-sleeve shirt my mother had ironed and laid out on my bed, hopped into yesterday's khaki pants, unrolled a pair of clean brown socks and laced up my brown school shoes before bounding down the staircase in the center of our house. I was so excited I don't remember my feet touching the stairs, as if I was floating like an angel, not that anyone I knew thought of me as one, certainly, nobody in my family. But I had this sense that I was as ready as I'd ever been to enter the big world outside of our neighborhood. Oh boy, was I ever ready!

Our neighborhood, the Beechwood Knoll, was on the marsh side of the Wollaston Beach boulevard that ran alongside Quincy Bay. Although the locals called the road 'the boulevard,' it was properly named Quincy Shore Drive and at a T-bone intersection with Fenno Street, it led into and beyond the knoll. I wouldn't have recognized a Beechwood tree unless I had a picture to go by, but the beach was another story. The beach looked like most other beaches I'd seen – magical – except it had rocks and stones where other beaches had sand. Sand would have been a definite improvement, but it was still a beach, still magical and it went on as far as I could see in both directions.

To the north, was the Boston skyline and slightly east of the skyline was Logan Airport where at busy times, the sky looked like a picture postcard of an approaching row of propeller passenger planes, spaced about two minutes apart, reminiscent of a parade of lumbering circus elephants. The planes appeared to move so slowly that it seemed like they might fall out of the sky before reaching the runway.

To the south was the bedroom neighborhood called Merrymount. Quincy had more residential neighborhoods than Dunkin' Donuts had doughnut flavors, speaking of which, the first ever Dunkin' Donuts shop opened on the Southern Artery in Quincy during the spring of 1950, about the same time as the field trip. I remember standing in a line outside the doughnut shop on a Friday evening during the grand opening, when the cost of a single doughnut was a nickel, and you could get a dozen for fifty-five cents.

Chapter Four

Kodachrome

When I got to the bottom of our staircase, the front door was open, a sure sign of warmer weather, and through the opening my mind captured a Kodachrome image of the outside world's picnic perfect, sky blue and shamrock green landscape. I could see the grey concrete sidewalks, islands of green grass, thin oak trees and grey concrete curb stones on both sides of Havilend Street's charcoal grey, asphalt surface. There, on weekday mornings, our Boston bound neighbors, dressed in business clothes, marched downhill toward the nearby bus stop, like two rows of ants heading for the melted remains of a cast-aside Baby Ruth candy bar wrapper.

Beyond the opposite sidewalk was a two-foot-high fieldstone retaining wall in front of the Smiths' house that kept their front lawn from washing away when it rained heavily because the slope was as steep as a schoolyard slide. My father said our house and Smiths' house were called center-entrance colonials. Smith's was #11 and was at the corner of Andrews Road. Ours was #10 and was at the corner of Dickens Street. Each house looked like a reflection of the other except that ours had a deck porch.

Watching Charlie Smith drive his car up their driveway was like watching a death-defying stunt at the

Norwood Demolition Derby, especially when his driveway was slick. In the four years I'd lived across the street, Charlie and his wife, Mildred, never had much to say to me, and most of our other neighbors were like that. My father, who had lived most of his life in New York City, said that was just the way people in New England behaved.

When you looked out our front door, downhill was to the right, and the corner bus stop was diagonally across the street, about half the length of a football field away. Picture it as though our front door was at the fifty-yard line and the bus stop was in the far end zone. It was the last stop on the Wollaston Beach line from Ashmont Station in Dorchester, from where our neighbors could catch a subway train to downtown Boston. Beyond the bus stop there was salt marsh as far as the eye could see. When puffs of wind caused the marsh grass to sway back and forth, the marsh looked like thousands of hula skirts, like ones I'd seen in a school movie about the Hawaiian Islands.

There were zillions of lately sprouted leaves on the trees and babbling, jabbering birds were fluttering around our front yard like the cage full of panicky yellow, green, purple and blue parakeets at Bowie's Pet Shop on Cottage Street in Quincy Center. Bowie's Pet Shop was my favorite store to visit. Whenever someone opened the door of the shop, a tiny bronze bell hanging on the inside jingled, and the parakeets started chirping like they were part of the girls' choir at a church. The star attraction was a Myna bird, as big, black and shiny as a raven, with a yellow stripe on its neck and orange beak, legs and feet. The bird could say, 'Hello, my name is Butch – one, two, four, five,' clear as day. How funny was that? A bird who was good at talking but bad at counting!

I went there whenever I could. Lester Bowie was a tall, thin, middle-aged man with thinning grey hair who usually wore plaid flannel shirts. He seemed to like explaining everything about tropical fish and exotic birds to kids and he never seemed to get tired of answering our idiotic questions about animals, even though most of the shop owners in Quincy Center didn't like having kids in their stores. Mr. Bowie, though, acted like the father every kid wanted – cool, calm, collected and caring. I never once heard him yell at any of us. He was the only guy who my friends and I thought was cool in spite of wearing a white plastic pocket protector for keeping ball point pens in his shirt. Usually, we called those guys geeks, but not good old Mr. Bowie. He was definitely cool.

Anyway, even the birds fluttering around our yard already knew something earthshaking was about to happen. They knew this was no ordinary spring day. This was a special day, and I was going with my class on a field trip to Fenway Park, home of the best baseball team ever. Good golly, how I loved those Red Sox!

This would be the day when Miss DiMascio's class from the Massachusetts Fields School would take a ten-mile, northbound magic carpet ride on the south wind from Wollaston to Boston. I'd been dying to watch the Sox play since we moved there in '46 because the team won the American League pennant that year and went on to play the St. Louis Cardinals in the World Series. That was what my new friends were talking about every day once school started.

You'd never know that Boston was also the home of the Braves, a National League team that played its games at a place called Braves Field, just over two miles from Fenway. My friends were Red Sox fans and that's all there was to it. My cousin, Catherine, was married to a man named Bill Leary, whose brother, Frank, was the travelling secretary for the Braves. I was hoping he'd give me a free ticket someday but that never happened. My father said Bill Leary was so tight that he squeaked and was also a blowhard so I shouldn't expect any favors from him no matter what he promised.

Anyway, this would be my first time to visit the inside of Fenway Park, and my first chance to see a Major League Baseball game in person. This was no small miracle either, mainly because of my mother, who I always figured would never let me go to a baseball game in Boston unless the pope sent a notarized letter of approval from the Vatican, hand delivered by Mr. Smalley, our mailman, or something similarly official.

I still recall that before I ran out the back door to head for school on the morning of the field trip, my mother was in the upstairs bathroom getting dressed up like she was planning to go somewhere special. When I asked her where she was going, she said, 'Oh, I don't know, maybe I'll catch a bus to Boston,' which she would usually do once or twice a month.

The walk from our house to school took fifteen minutes, passed Sailors' Home Pond and crossed through the campus of Eastern Nazarene College. Our school was a two-story, brown brick building on Beach Street, across from Mac's Variety Store or as one of the kids called it, 'Mac's Varlies,' a goofy name that somehow stuck. There was another kid who called the convenience store on the adjacent corner, the 'Untied' Market, instead of the United Market. Some of the things I remember from back then are really weird; maybe that's why I remember them.

When I got to my desk on the second floor, the first things I noticed were the hands on the classroom wall clock above the front chalk board. They seemed like they were moving in slow motion. Even the second hand seemed to take a full minute to go from number one to number two. I wasn't paying much attention to Miss DiMascio. Whatever she was saying sounded like she was half asleep, but she was a great teacher, my favorite, and it seemed like everyone in the class liked her.

According to my mother, Miss DiMascio was an 'old maid' because she'd never been married. But she didn't look old to me, maybe middle-age, with short black hair. She wasn't fat or thin, she was right in the middle. She wasn't beautiful or ugly, either, again right in the middle. And she had a terrific smile, liked to laugh and never seemed to get angry, even with me, and that's saying a lot because my mother used to say to me all the time, 'You'd try the patience of a saint.'

Nothing was moving fast enough for my liking, so I

volunteered to be the lookout for the bus that was coming to get us. I peered out of the tall second-story classroom windows, the ones that rattled like crazy in the wind. I had to use a wooden pole with a brass hook on the end to open and close the windows because the latches were way up near the ceiling, thanks to the four-foot-high brown radiators that were bolted into the floor. In the cold weather, we had to be careful not to touch the radiators when we walked past them because they got hot enough to make your skin sizzle like bacon frying. The window pole reminded me of the brass gismo I had to use to light and snuff out the candles at St. Ann's Church when I was learning to be an altar boy.

I liked being in charge of opening and closing the windows at school, but I hated being an altar boy because I couldn't remember the Latin phrases to save my life. I'd say whatever came to my mind in Pig Latin until Father Daily figured out that I was talking gibberish. That was the day when, instead of saying the correct Latin response, 'et cum spiritu tuo,' I said something like 'earhay umscay ethey iritspay ootay.' Father Daily stopped what he was doing, gave me a quizzical look, ordered me to repeat what I'd just said only louder so everyone could hear me. When I did there was plenty of laughter, including his. Funny or not, that ended my career as an altar boy. You can only imagine how my mother felt about me getting tossed out of the altar boys program on my ear.

I stood, by the windows, waiting for our transportation to the ball game, inspecting the roofs of the passing vehicles until I spied the long white roof of the dark green Eastern Mass. Street Railway Company bus. Once I knew we were actually going to Fenway Park to see the Red Sox, I focused on every instruction Miss DiMascio uttered, to be sure I didn't get left behind.

I couldn't imagine anything better, not even a trunk full of DC comic books, Topps baseball cards, cap pistols, squirt guns, rolls of caps, pea shooters, lead soldiers, punk firecrackers, Duncan yo-yos, Lincoln Logs, Lionel trains and balsa wood planes. If I had been any more excited, I'd have probably exploded like a party balloon that got too close to a birthday candle.

Speaking of pea shooters, there was nothing that would sting human flesh as sharply as one of those dried split peas. My sisters hated me whenever I'd zing a dried pea off one of their arms or the back of their necks. Once, Barbara threatened to kill me if I ever did it again. My mother solved that problem by grabbing my pea shooter and breaking it in half. Jimmy told me later that it was a good thing for me that I never shot him because he'd have stuffed the pea shooter in one ear so hard it would have come out my other ear. Yikes!

Chapter Five

Love on a bus

It was time to go. We boarded the bus, rocking it from side to side under the weight and movement of all of us, until everyone found a seat, mine on the aisle about halfway back. I was ready to explode with excitement over taking a bus ride to watch Major League Baseball, but I definitely was not prepared to fall in love on a bus.

But my classmate, Molly Noonan, scooted in beside me and sat down next to the window. Normally she sat behind me in class, and now she was seated next to me. She smiled at me. I think I smiled too. Imagine my luck, sitting next to Molly Noonan with her long, honey-brown hair and fabulous smile. Molly Noonan, easily the cutest girl in my class. I had a huge crush on her despite not even knowing then what a crush was. Molly had a look about her like Snow White in a Disney movie. She had light pink skin, rosy cheeks and a smile that looked like it was painted by that famous artist, Norman Rockwell, whose paintings were on the covers of The Saturday Evening Post magazines every week.

Molly was adorable and cuddly, although I'd never cuddled with her because I was too shy to try anything that daring with a girl. I didn't know what it was about her, but in 5th grade Molly for me was like a soft light in

a dark room or a gentle fire on a cold night. Knowing Molly was sitting behind me in class made me feel good – like the world was right. It wasn't that we talked a lot or did things together; it was just that I felt good because she was there, as though she belonged there. Whenever I looked at her, she seemed to be smiling at me, which embarrassed me to the point of turning red. I'd think, 'Why would a pretty girl be smiling at me?' I had no explanation other than the realization that I was happier when Molly was near me. Things just seemed better when she was around. I didn't get it, and I was afraid to let on to anyone, especially Molly, that I liked her more than any other girl I'd ever met. She was very special even if I wasn't sure why.

Once in a while in class I'd turn sideways to sneak a peek at her. If she caught me, she'd smile and ask if I needed something. I'd make up some alibi about, say, trying to get a better look at something on the side wall, like the examples of cursive writing. Or I'd deliberately drop my pencil in Molly's direction so she might pick it up and tap me on the shoulder, which would allow me a brief, inconspicuous glimpse of her.

I'd also try to look nice when I got dressed for school so that Molly wouldn't think I was a slob. And because she sat right behind me, I made sure that the skin on the back of my neck and behind my ears was scrubbed clean. I concluded that I was losing my marbles and did what any red-blooded kid would have done – I pretended I didn't give a hoot about Molly and ignored her as much as I could to keep anyone from suspecting what I felt for her.

Who knew what a ten-year-old kid was supposed to do with a girl anyway? Who knew that a ten-year-old kid could fall in love on a bus? Who knew that a 10-year-old kid could turn into a blithering idiot because sitting next to a pretty girl thrilled him? I was so smitten with Molly Noonan that it was difficult for me, at that moment, to believe that a Red Sox baseball game could be more exciting than being with her. This was all new stuff to me. Before the bus ride, about the only feeling I ever had about women was being scared to death of my mother, my two older sisters and the nuns in Park Ridge.

And then on the bus, the most astonishing thing happened – Molly slipped her hand into mine! WOW! Talk about an attack of goose bumps!

I thought I was daydreaming, but I wasn't. Her hand was definitely warm, and it smelled like Ivory soap. Was it the Ivory soap aroma that made my face flush; made my skin get hot all over? Or, crazy as it seemed, was it Molly? What the heck was wrong with me anyway? A voice inside my head said, 'Get a grip on yourself, Murph, before you turn into a looney.' I thought it was the voice of God, or my father, which was pretty much the same thing.

This was a groundbreaking moment for me, never to be forgotten, even though, until that time, I had the opinion that most girls were disgusting. And it wasn't just because I had sisters. I'd formed that opinion the morning that my classmate, Julie Kirkland, who sat on my left in Miss DiMascio's class, leaned toward me to ask if we could kiss sometime. I looked at her face and saw she had mustard on her upper lip. Mustard? Who eats mustard for breakfast? I thought it must have been left over from supper. Maybe she'd been eating franks and Boston baked beans. I wondered if she'd even washed her face or brushed her teeth.

Although I hadn't planned it, I couldn't stop myself from blurting out, 'What, are you, nuts?' Then this weird look came over her like she was becoming cross-eyed, and, with an explosion, she vomited on the floor between our desks. If that wasn't bad enough, she had the nerve to say it was my fault – she puked because I made her panicky! Try explaining that while you're rinsing off your shoes in the boys' bathroom.

But while holding Molly's hand, I certainly felt something I'd never felt before – a warm sensation all over from being touched by a girl. My face felt like I was lying in the hot sun on Wollaston Beach, and I was becoming delirious enough to think that Molly might actually like me if she wanted to hold my hand, in public no less. I felt like a Hollywood movie star or a sports celebrity. I suddenly had a sense of importance that was exhilarating. Who knew that something as simple as holding hands with the cutest girl in the class would transform my mind from that of a child to one of a man?

I barely had time to figure out what was going on before my bubble burst. I spied, out of the corner of my eye, the most terrifying, perilous hazard I could have imagined. One that was entering the bus just as it was getting ready to pull away from the school. One that made me wonder if I'd really seen what I thought I saw. One that made fear run up and down my spine like I had a life-threatening case of the chilly willies or the heebie jeebies.

One of the kids near the front of the bus yelled out sarcastically, 'Hey, Murph, your mother's here, good luck to you.' My first thought was 'Holy crap, that's the last thing I need right now.' If I hadn't believed it before the kid announced it, I sure did afterwards. I became scared and angry at the same time. I was afraid that my mother was coming to drag me off the bus for having done something wrong, like not finishing breakfast or not making my bed the correct way or holding hands with Molly. But I had made double sure I'd finished my breakfast, every last Cheerio, and since Molly had just started holding my hand, how could my mother have known about it unless she had x-ray vision or ESP?

So, there I am, staring at my mother, who's wearing dress-up clothes and that's when I began to put two and two together. Her arrival wasn't just any coincidence. Miss DiMascio must have invited her to go to the game or maybe my mother invited herself. Yeah, that was more like it – she invited herself. My mother of all people. Maybe my teacher and my mother were in cahoots. Holding hands with Molly and going to a Red Sox game could not have been more exciting. But now I was terrified because my mother was coming along.

One thing seemed sure – Miss DiMascio didn't realize that my mother was a housewife who hardly ever left home. Her usual daily attire was a housedress and sometimes an apron. More often than not she covered her hair with a bandana, like the one worn by

Aunt Jemima on the pancake boxes. We only had one car and Adelaide Healey Murphy, my mother, didn't have a license to drive. The closest thing to driving she did was steer her Kirby vacuum cleaner through the house. She was proud of it because it had a headlight and rubber bumpers but, somehow, the wooden legs of our furniture looked like they had been in an automobile accident. My guess was that was why my father refused to let her learn to drive his big black Buick. He was very protective of that car.

Why in the world would Miss DiMascio have done something that ridiculous and why hadn't she warned me that my mother was coming? For that matter, why hadn't my mother told me she was coming? Why was that a secret? It seemed like I was always the last one in my family to know anything. I lived in a world of secrets. I hated that part of my life. This was a perfect example of what was wrong with my life – I wasn't leading it. I was following the life my mother planned for me, right down to how my hair was parted.

And here she was, my mother of all people, going on the bus ride to Fenway with my 5th grade class. I felt like the long arm of the law was reaching inside the bus to grab me. But she hadn't walked back to where I was sitting yet or even made eye contact with me. Suddenly, it dawned on me why she had allowed me to go to the game in the first place. She had finagled a way to be a chaperone just so she could keep an eye on me, probably both eyes.

Certainly, it couldn't have been because she liked baseball. I'd have bet two-bits, a box of caps, my spare yo-yo string and all of my duplicate Red Sox baseball trading cards that my mother didn't have any idea of what baseball was about. I'd never heard her, my father, or my sisters talk about baseball. My older brother was the only one who seemed to care about baseball, but I could barely understand anything he said about it because he had such a severe speech impediment.

I was already jumpy enough without worrying about what bizarre thing my mother would do to embarrass Molly and me during the bus ride over. I decided the best plan would be to pretend that I didn't know either one of them, Molly or my mother. Was my mother trying to ruin my life? What cool kid brings his mother along on anything this important? No cool kid, that's who. I wondered how life could get much worse.

So, I pulled my hand away before Molly could be humiliated by my mother's third-degree interrogation, and there definitely would have been one, starting with what church Molly attended and what her father did for a living. When I took my hand away, Molly's smile turned upside-down and, judging by her gloomy expression, I knew I had insulted her. We didn't speak the rest of the way to Fenway.

I was vibrating with excitement but suddenly I had nobody to share it with. I was already dreading the aftermath of the hand-holding incident. I figured Molly would probably never talk to me again and I couldn't blame her. I concluded that romance might be one of those things that was 'easy come, easy go.'

I wanted to explain to Molly about my mother's

behavior, but I was scared that she'd start crying, or sock me in the nose, in which case I'd start crying. That wouldn't have been a good look or a proud moment for me, so I dummied up and made believe she didn't exist. Boy, was that a mistake! I've never forgotten about Molly. I know now that I must have actually fallen in love on that dark green bus.

How in the world was that possible? I'd never been in love with a girl, and I knew darn well that no girl had ever been in love with me. There were so many things that I knew nothing about that it was embarrassing. And, love, especially love, was at the top of the list. Sure, I loved baseball but that was way different than loving a girl. I enjoyed baseball and understood the rules. That wasn't true about girls. Girls seemed to me to be troublesome, confusing, unpredictable and capable of deep emotional feelings. I didn't understand any of the rules for dealing with them, especially Molly Noonan.

Chapter Six

Jersey Street

We arrived at Fenway Park more than an hour before game time, but we had to stay on the bus for a bit until Miss DiMascio lectured us about the Fenway Park neighborhood. Before we debussed, she told us that Fenway Park was located in a section of Boston called the Back Bay. She leaned against the pedestal that held the fare box beside the bus driver's seat and faced us while she talked. According to her, the neighborhood had been known as 'The Fens,' until the 'city fathers' decided to fill in enough marsh to build the ballpark, some yellow brick apartment buildings and a handful of shops.

She told us the neighborhood was named Kenmore Square and that Fenway Park's postal address was #4 Jersey Street where the main entrance to the park was located and where fans could buy tickets for seats. I couldn't believe it cost only $1.60 for a grandstand seat. What a bargain that was! I seemed to be the only guy on the bus who hadn't been to Fenway before, and my mother had told me that was because the price of tickets was too expensive. I thought she meant it was like $10 or some other enormous amount, not $1.60. Jeez, wasn't I worth a buck-sixty?

It seemed to me that Miss DiMascio would never stop gabbing because I was dying to get inside the ballpark. Nevertheless, she wanted us to know that some of the nearby streets ran parallel to each other and had alphabetical names of some British noblemen at the time Boston was being built. Names like Arlington, Berkeley, Clarendon, Dartmouth, Exeter, Fairfield, Gloucester, Hereford, Ipswich, Jersey, Kilmarnock and Lansdowne. I never knew that street names could be alphabetical and didn't really care much, either. My father, James Augustine Murphy, Sr., was always trying to impress other people with trivial information. As far as I was concerned, it should have been called useless information, but I decided I'd give my father some of his own medicine by memorizing the alphabetical street names and reciting them to him when I got home. Little did I know that he already knew every one of them in exact order.

From the outside, Fenway Park didn't look at all like I'd expected. It looked more like the old red brick warehouse building at Roxbury Crossing that was owned by my cousin, Arch MacLellan. It reminded me of some historical place, like a museum. But when we walked inside, I was struck by sounds unlike any I'd ever heard. 'Scorecahds, getcha Red Sox scorecahds!' someone called out. 'Cold beah heah!' And then, 'hotdogs, getcha red-hot hotdogs!' A hotdog vendor, wearing a Red Sox cap backward, said the hotdogs were 'wicked good,' a Boston term I'd never heard before. There were more new sights and sounds there than I'd ever encountered in one place before and I was all eyes and ears.

Then a cart stuffed with all kinds of souvenirs caught my eye. I desperately wanted one of the large red and blue Red Sox pennants to hang on the bedroom wall above my pillow but my father wouldn't allow me to put holes in the plaster, so I quickly forgot about that idea. If you had seen how big my father was, you'd know what I'm talking about. But I wasn't desperate enough to ask my mother to buy me anything. That would not have been a smart move. It wasn't just that she'd probably refuse, but I knew I wouldn't be able to take the humiliation she'd put me through because she had no idea of what being a kid was like.

As the class walked inside the brick wall enclosing the ballpark, there was a ramp that went downward to an open area called a concourse beneath the grandstand seats. There, people wearing white uniforms were cooking hamburgers, hot dogs and sausages with sizzling smells and the lines of people waiting to buy beer looked like the traffic jam we'd been in as our bus was approaching the ballpark.

Miss DiMascio led us up a different ramp, this one behind home plate. That was where I caught my first view of the ball field. The sight was absolutely breathtaking. I actually gasped! I'd been to the Ringling Brothers, Barnum & Bailey Circus at the Boston Garden when I was in 4th grade. That had been the most spectacular thing I'd ever seen until Fenway Park. But the sun-bright ballfield at Fenway was way better... even better than lions, tigers and elephants! Who'd have ever thought that was possible?

Walking out from the shade into the brilliant sunshine was like watching a theatre curtain rising, revealing the world's biggest, brightest stage. I had gone once to something called a minstrel show at North Quincy High School and remembered how flabbergasted I was when the stage curtain parted and the entire cast was standing on stage, flooded by bright white light. When the minstrel show started, there was ear-popping music, singing and dancing. I saw sights I'd never dreamed about including white men dressed in old-fashioned clothing and wearing black greasepaint on their faces, so they'd look like dark folks. I'd never seen anything so ridiculous and exciting at the same time. I didn't much like Southern music but something about that music and the dancing was special, and I found myself singing along and tapping my right foot like I was on stage.

But this wasn't a high school stage. This was Fenway Park, and I stood staring at the sunlit grass, such a vibrant shade of green that it made me feel as though I'd just entered the Emerald City in the wonderful land of Oz. The dirt in the infield diamond had a reddish-brown color like a color picture I'd seen of tobacco fields in North Carolina, and it looked as smooth as beach sand on the ocean side of Cape Cod. There were colorful billboards around the stadium and music coming through loudspeakers. More calls for 'cold beah heah' and hotdogs and peanuts sounded almost like singing. Fenway looked like a magical garden with tens of thousands of dark green wooden seats surrounding the field.

Ballplayers were sprinting across the outfield. Groundskeepers began watering the infield. and through the mist from their hoses the wet grass shimmered like lime Jell-O. The puffy white clouds floating overhead reminded me of whipped cream. Who would have ever thought that my first view of Fenway Park would look anything like lime Jell-O and whipped cream?

The sunlight created a rainbow through the mist from the hoses. It was almost like I was in The Wizard of Oz, and I could hear Judy Garland singing 'Somewhere Over the Rainbow.' A flavor of fantasy and a spirit of enchantment made me feel like I was in some other world. Yet we were only about a half-hour away from Wollaston Beach. I was getting giddier by the second. I felt as though my fairy godmother had tapped me on the shoulder with a magic wand and I began reciting, 'Abracadabra, alakazam, Fenway Park, here I am.' My mother had a saying about being in amazing places: 'Who'da thunk it?' I can assure you that I'd never thunk that I'd be anywhere like Fenway Park!

I'd heard about the wall in left field, the one called the 'Green Monster.' Its name made the ballpark sound mysterious, like some place in a Brothers Grimm fairy tale. But the monster wasn't as bright a shade of green as the grass. It was more like the dark green color of the bus we came on. Someone said that the wall was thirty-seven feet high. To me it looked like a whole building with a giant net on top, big enough to catch Moby Dick.

Someone had said there were dents in the wall from getting hit by baseballs all the time. I couldn't see any from my seat behind home plate, more than 300 feet away. I thought about craters on the moon that I'd seen in a photograph on the back cover of Life magazine and wondered what the wall was made of if it could be dented by baseballs. Maybe it was made of green cheese like some people said about the moon.

Near the bottom of this dark and foreboding wall was a scoreboard where, incredibly, men from inside the wall were sticking their heads through the rectangular openings where numbers were supposed to go. It looked like something from a Three Stooges movie. I laughed out loud, never expecting that going to a ballgame would be as comical as watching Moe, Larry and Curly.

Hovering above the grandstands, there were flat roofs, also dark green, that framed a horseshoe-shape sky, blue and white, more brilliant than the night-time movie screen at the Neponset Drive-In Theater after dark. Some of the clouds, the wispy ones, drifted above my right shoulder toward the outfield, reminding me of my father's cigar smoke. Everything I noticed about Fenway Park amazed me. And the baseball game hadn't even started yet!

Men carried food and drinks in big cases with neck straps or shoulder straps right to where we were sitting, and we passed things down the row of seats whenever someone bought something. Then money got passed in the other direction to pay the guy selling the food. It quickly became annoying if you were sitting in an aisle seat, as I was. But what was more annoying was when someone toward the middle of the row had to use one of the public toilets and half the row had to stand up to let the person out... then in again.

My mother was sitting at the other end of my row. I'd been trying to avoid looking in her direction, fearful that she'd wave to me and holler something embarrassing. It didn't work, though and soon came those dreaded singsong words, 'Yoo-hoo, Bobby!' Ugh, there it was. She'd called me Bobby in front of my school friends, not to mention the 'Yoo-hoo!' That was all I had to hear to pretend that I didn't know her.

She asked my classmates sitting between us to find

out if I wanted something to eat or drink. Her outburst made me feel more like hiding under my seat than eating. I kept staring straight ahead, like I hadn't heard a word she'd said. Suddenly a crumpled, balled-up dollar bill arrived from the other end of the row. I knew it was from my mother because I could smell her perfume and see the beige powder that usually spilled inside her pocketbook, which was more like a small suitcase, crammed with a wallet, perfume bottle, lipstick tube, powder container, mirror, nail file and who-knew-what-else.

I used the dollar to buy a hotdog and a Coke and passed the change down the row to her. I knew that a Coke was a Coke wherever I bought it, but I soon found out that a ballgame hotdog was better than practically any other hotdog anywhere, except maybe the kind served in grilled, buttered rolls at Howard Johnson's roadside restaurants, the places with the orange roofs and orange steeples. Grilling a hotdog roll in butter made a big difference to me. Actually, buttering almost all food was one thing, maybe the only thing, that my mother and I agreed about.

I could see fans in brightly colored clothing flowing up and down the aisles in the centerfield bleachers and in the right field stands behind where the pitchers were warming up. I was amazed by the constant buzzing noise the crowd made. It sounded like the swarm of bees in the hollow place in the trunk of our backyard linden tree whenever the squirrels stirred them up.

The sounds were thrilling, the sights were stupendous. The aromas were delicious. The excitement was contagious. I was so anxious for the game to begin that I couldn't sit still. When the Red Sox players were introduced over the public address system, the crowd went totally berserk, hooting and whistling like a bunch of maniacs and I was one of those maniacs.

Chapter Seven

Teddy Ballgame

'Ladies and gentlemen, boys and girls, introducing your hometown Boston Red Sox,' came the announcement over the loudspeakers.

The sound of the crowd cheering might have been deafening if the ballpark had been full but there were less fans there than I had expected. Someone said that fewer fans came to weekday afternoon games because most men were at work, which made sense to me. As I looked around, it was obvious that there were fewer women than men. It wasn't even close. The night before the game I'd asked my father how many baseball games he'd gone to in his life and was shocked when he said, 'None.' Thinking about his answer, I felt really sad that although he had lived in New York City, Chicago and Boston he had never seen what I was seeing. Sure, he would have worn a white shirt, a floral tie and a straw Panama hat but I would have felt good about him being there just the same. But, let's face it,

Ted Williams was who I most wanted to see. Ted Williams, better known to my friends and me as Teddy Ballgame; that name was magical.

The next announcement was: 'Leading off and playing centerfield, #23, Clyyyyde Vollmerrrr.'

The big crowd roared again, but not me! Something was horribly wrong because I had no idea who this Clyde guy was or how to spell his name. But I did know he wasn't supposed to be the leadoff batter, or the centerfielder. He wasn't even supposed to be playing. I'd listened to enough Red Sox games on the white plastic RCA table model radio beside my bed to know that I was missing a chance to see someone important, and I felt like I was getting gypped.

Everyone knew that Dom DiMaggio was supposed to be the leadoff batter for the Red Sox, and that his nickname was The Little Professor because he was small, studious looking and wore eyeglasses. I didn't know of any other ballplayers who wore glasses. My friends called Dom's brother, Joe, a dirty rat because he played for the New York Yankees, the dreaded Bronx Bombers. There were those who said that Joe was as good a hitter as Ted Williams, but I didn't believe it. Nobody could be as good at hitting a baseball as Ted. Nobody. But out of respect for Joe DiMaggio's ability, I once heard Ted say in an interview that Joe was the 'best right-handed hitter in baseball.' Of course, Bostonians who followed baseball knew that Ted was the best left-handed hitter and a better hitter overall than Joe DiMaggio.

So, I thought the top of the Red Sox batting order

would be Dom DiMaggio, Johnny Pesky, Ted Williams, followed by Vern Stephens, Bobby Doerr and the rookie, Walt Dropo. I was pretty sure it was the best batting order in all of baseball. I wanted to know why Dom DiMaggio wasn't playing and why Bobby Doerr was batting seventh, but I didn't know who to ask.

During the player introductions, the fans kept screaming with joy. Fenway Park was the first place I could remember where you could shout at the top of your lungs without getting into trouble. When the Red Sox came out of the 1st base dugout, I couldn't believe how big some of them were – as big as my father. I'd never before seen grown men playing baseball, except in Movietone News at the Wollaston Theatre, aka the 'Wolly,' where the players' legs always looked like they were moving faster than they were supposed to move.

In person, the Sox players looked kind of odd at first because their uniforms looked like baggy, white flannel pyjamas with big red numbers on the backs. I was studying the numbers, trying to figure out who was who, since I didn't have a program. Mostly I was looking for #9, the number worn by Ted Williams.

The announcer then asked everyone to join in singing the National Anthem. We all stood up. Although I purposely didn't look at Molly, who was at the right end of the row in front of me. I couldn't help but wonder whether she was holding another guy's hand instead of mine.

Men wearing hats took them off. People held their right hands over their hearts. The whole place got really quiet before the organ music started. Even the ballplayers took their caps off and faced the flagpole in centerfield. It was a time when people felt proud to be Americans. Of course, at school we pledged allegiance to the flag every morning, but the ballpark ceremony was way more impressive, and, at Fenway, nobody checked to make sure we were holding our right hands over our hearts. At school, you could get sent to the principal's office for not holding your hand over your heart. And another thing, if you were assigned to take down the huge American flag that was flown from the pole on the school's front lawn, you had to be sure not to let the flag touch the ground, or you could get kept after school for punishment. In the world I lived in, the two most respected symbols were the Catholic crucifix and the American flag.

I remember once, after memorizing the Pledge of Allegiance at school, asking my father during supper who was this man named Richard Stanz. My father asked me where I'd heard about him, and I said his name was in the Pledge of Allegiance where it says, '... and to the republic for Richard Stanz.' The laughter was humiliating.

Then came the public address announcer yelling into his microphone, 'Play ball!'

The Red Sox were playing against the visiting St. Louis Browns. Boston's starting pitcher was Chuck Stobbs, a lefty. I had hoped that the starting pitcher would be the Sox' best pitcher, Mel Parnell, another lefty, but no such luck. Stobbs threw the first pitch, and I heard it hit the catcher's mitt and I saw a puff of dust come out. But I never quite saw the ball. It went so unbelievably fast it was practically invisible and the dust might actually have been smoke for all I knew.

I always thought I was a pretty good hitter, but I knew I couldn't have hit that pitch, even if I had brought my Louisville Slugger bat, the one that used to belong to my brother Jimmy until he cracked the thing. Even though I'd hammered short nails into the barrel of the bat and wrapped it in black electrical tape for good measure, it would have smashed to smithereens if by dumb luck I happened to hit something. A Brooklyn Dodger outfielder named Duke Snider once instructed kids, 'Swing hard in case they're throwing the ball where you're swinging.'

It soon became obvious to me and everyone in the ballpark that by the bottom of the 2nd inning, Parnell wouldn't be needed. Nor would any other Boston pitcher be needed that day. And with all due respect to the great Dodger centerfielder, it didn't matter how hard the Browns swung. They were no match for the home team's pitcher.

I should have guessed that Ted Williams would hit the first home run of the game; it happened in the bottom of the 2nd inning. It happened so fast it looked like he'd hardly swung at the pitch and the ball was launched off his bat like a WWII German V-2 rocket. It startled the crowd to its feet and caused us to make a gasping sound, like everyone was inhaling at once. Actually, the ball looked more like a shooting star that appeared above home plate, shot over the field, and disappeared into the rightfield stands as though dropping beyond the earth's horizon.

I knew that Teddy Ballgame was famous for hitting home runs, but I never guessed that he would hit two of them that day and that there'd be five more hit by other Red Sox players. I also never guessed that Ted would come to bat twice in the 2nd inning, and that the Sox would score eight runs in the inning. And that was just a sign of things to come.

Bobby Doerr hit three home runs in the game. Whack! Whack! Whack! Some players couldn't hit three home runs in an entire season. The sound of a wooden bat hitting a baseball echoed throughout the ballpark like it was being played over the loudspeakers. Doerr drove in eight runs. Walt Dropo hit two homers and drove in seven runs. Williams knocked in five runs on the day. Those three players hit seven home runs and knocked in twenty runs between them. Imagine me watching Ted Williams, Teddy Ballgame, The Splendid Splinter, The Kid, #9, hit two home runs during my first ever game. How lucky could I get?

Nor did I ever guess, before getting to Fenway, how far a baseball had to travel to become a home run. Not only was the left field wall thirty-seven feet high but it might as well have been the side of a two-story building. There was a corner in centerfield that was so far away from home plate that it looked like it might have been part of the next town, Brookline, and the bleacher seats above it were nearly as high as the left field screen. In right field, a ball had to land in one of the two bullpens or go over them to be a homer and those right field stands looked like I'd need binoculars to see where a ball landed out there. And those seats were where

Teddy Ballgame hit most of his 'round-trippers,' as Jim Britt, the radio announcer, called home runs.

Somehow, Ted Williams seemed different from the other players, but I couldn't put my finger on exactly what the difference was. It was more than how he looked and how he played the game. It was something magical, something I sensed when I saw him on the field, something that made the crowd roar like a lion when his name was announced. It was something like seeing a rainbow over the Cape Cod Canal at the end of an August thunderstorm. Or being touched by the sun's rays at dawn on the peak of Mount Washington, New Hampshire. Or being warmed by the brilliant glow from one of my father's Christmas tree extravaganzas.

When Williams came up to bat, he had so much swagger that he stood out from all the other players. When he swung the bat, he looked as smooth as a downhill skier on fresh, fluffy snow. The other players were more herky-jerky than Ted. He was as graceful as a figure skater at Sailors' Home Pond, a ballroom dancer at the Nantasket Beach pavilion, or a seagull gliding back and forth on a puff of summer air above Quincy Bay.

I used to admire my brother Jimmy, when he played hockey at Sailors' Home Pond; I hoped that someday I'd be as good an athlete as him but that would never happen. How effortless his motions seemed on the glistening white ice, and Ted's movements had a similar appearance on the shimmering green grass. I was proud to be Jimmy's kid brother and I was proud to be a Ted Williams fan. I decided that I wanted to meet Teddy Ballgame more than General Douglas MacArthur, President Harry Truman and the Pope, none of whom I ever expected to meet, least of all Williams.

Of all the players I saw, Ted was the smoothest and when he jogged in from left field at the end of an inning, his head bobbed up and down like a racehorse I'd seen on a newsreel about the Kentucky Derby. The fans cheered louder for Ted than anyone else. He was definitely everyone's hero, but I'm pretty sure I was the first one to ever call him 'the hero of Jersey Street.'

And if Ted Williams wasn't famous enough as a ballplayer, his time as a Navy pilot during WWII made him more famous and the fact that he looked as much like a movie star as John Wayne, made it even better – he definitely was my hero, especially now that I'd seen him in person. Yesiree, there couldn't be another hero anywhere that could hold a candle to Teddy Ballgame, not in my mind anyway.

The Red Sox slaughtered the hapless Browns that day by a score of 29-4; at the time it was the most lopsided big league baseball score of all time. If you don't believe me, you can look it up: June 8, 1950, and I was there.

Chapter Eight

Like A Zombie

I don't know how it happened, but after the game I wound up wandering around the concrete concourse under the stands, like a zombie. I can't remember how I got there. I must have zigged when the rest of my class zagged. I think I got confused trying to discover where the ballplayers went after the game, maybe so I could get some autographs, but I couldn't figure it out. I didn't have any paper, or a pen anyway, so how was I supposed to get autographs?

I couldn't figure out where my classmates had gone. How could that have happened? Didn't anyone realize I was missing? Didn't Miss DiMascio have a list with everyone's name on it? Didn't my mother realize her own kid was absent from the group?

My mother had intentionally abandoned me once in Marshall Field's department store in Chicago when I was about five, which was the most frightening day in my life until then. Next, she abandoned me with a couple in Park Ridge who I'd never met before which caused more fright. Had she done it again at Fenway Park in Boston? There were only about thirty people on the field trip. How could they have lost someone and not have known about it?

My mind was still running wild with memories of baseballs flying around the park like there had been a nine-inning snowball fight, players repeatedly circling the bases like they were on a never-ending merry-go-round and fans jumping up and down like swarms of startled grasshoppers.

Don't ask me how I got lost because it was all a blur. Part of the reason might have been that the concourses under the stands looked the same from one place to another and there were thousands of fans leaving all at once. But when I realized the ballpark was practically empty, I started to get panicky because I knew I'd probably get in worse trouble for getting lost at Fenway Park than for any of the other dumb things I'd done in my life. This one could have been way worse.

One of the Fenway ushers, a young guy with red hair, freckles and glasses with clear plastic frames, guessed that I was lost. I remember his glasses because my uncle Eddie wore glasses just like them. The usher stopped and wanted to take me to an office somewhere to call my mother or father. I convinced him that I wasn't lost and that I was waiting for my mother to come out of the nearby public toilet. The guy finally went away. It wasn't long afterward that I really was alone. I remember being afraid I'd get locked inside the stadium for the night and that my parents would have to send the Boston Police or the United States Army to search for me. I imagined Army trucks with huge spotlights being driven into the stadium. I thought about police cars driving around with loudspeakers so the cops could call out, 'Bobby Murphy, come out wherever you are!' I could just see my parents fuming during the 11 o'clock news on channel 4 if the lead story was about me being a missing person.

That was when I first heard it – a sharp, cracking noise like the time an enormous branch in the center of our linden tree snapped during a hurricane. Or when I fell through the ice at the pond after my sister Barbara deliberately shoved me onto a place that the other kids said wasn't safe. An echo made it difficult to locate the source of the noise until I realized there was a guy aiming a rifle from the dirt area in front of the Red Sox dugout and shooting toward the sky as he slowly pivoted in a circle. The rifle wasn't much bigger than my brother's BB rifle except that the barrel and the stock were longer. The next shot resulted in something falling into the seats behind the dugout. It took one more shot before I realized that the guy was shooting at pigeons that were flying around the ballpark. How crazy was that?

The shooting continued as each shot spooked some of the birds that were perched on the steel beams holding up the roofs. When the birds took off, the guy with the rifle shot one or two of them out of the air like they were German Messerschmitt fighter planes or Japanese Kamikaze dive bombers. Who would have guessed that someone would be shooting pigeons above Kenmore Square on a warm weekday afternoon in June?

I was curious about who might be shooting pigeons inside Fenway Park. When I made my way through a chest-high green gate between home plate and third base, I started walking across the grass between me and the shooter without realizing I might be doing something stupid. It never occurred to me that the guy with the rifle might have hated kids and decided to shoot me.

I noticed some workers in the outfield putting equipment inside a huge garage door opening in the center field wall but there was nobody close enough to protect me except one usher stationed behind the first base dugout. But he seemed to have his hands full, collecting dead pigeons and putting them into a white canvas bag with a drawstring that looked like the clothespins bag on my mother's clothesline, where she hung our laundry out to dry every Monday, weather permitting.

It was then I recognized the shooter, even without his Red Sox uniform – tall, thin, good looking, with a full head of brown wavy hair. He wore a tan sport jacket, a white shirt with a long open collar lying on top of the lapels of the jacket and dark brown pleated slacks, with brown and white shoes that looked like a pair my father wore. The shooter's waist was so slim that I thought it must have been why people sometimes called him The Splendid Splinter, even though his shoulders looked pretty wide and square. I learned later that the splendid splinter was a reference to his bat, not him.

When I got a few feet closer, he turned to go into the dugout and, at that moment, he spotted me. He stopped in his tracks and so did I. He stared at me but said nothing. I was stunned and I said nothing. I'd heard that he didn't talk much to people, especially newspaper reporters and fans. Imagine me, all by myself, standing

close enough to Ted Williams that if I said anything he'd hear me. I could have spoken to him, but I was frozen with fear and had no idea what to say anyway.

He started back down the steps into the dugout before stopping and turning toward me again. This time he spoke. 'Hey kid,' he said, 'where are you supposed to be?'

His voice was so deep, smooth and clear, better than the announcer Jim Britt, more like some crooner like Bing Crosby, or even John Wayne, my favorite cowboy actor. His face and hands were tan even though it was only June. He had to be the handsomest person I'd ever seen as well as the best hitter ever, and to have been a Navy fighter pilot in addition was amazing. It was too much for me to comprehend all at once.

This was my big chance to talk to him, but my tongue was paralysed, stuck to the roof of my mouth, like in one of those terrifying nightmares where you try to scream for help but only groaning sounds come out. It was as though someone had stapled my lips shut or put a golf ball inside my mouth, or both. I was trying so hard to say something impressive, anything at all, that it was like having speech constipation. I just wanted to cry because I couldn't say a word. Not even one gosh-darned word.

I felt like such a moron. It was the chance of a lifetime, and I was blowing it. If I had just asked him for his autograph, maybe my friends might believe that I'd met this great ballplayer, but without it nobody was going to believe my story about meeting Ted Williams. In fact, since I didn't say anything to him and didn't even shake his hand, how could I say that I'd met him? All I could say was that I'd seen him, up close in his street clothes, holding a rifle in his hands after shooting some pigeons out of the sky. But who the heck would believe that crazy story?

Before I could do anything, or get my mouth to work, Ted disappeared into the shadows of what looked like a tunnel at the back of the dugout. I was so upset, so ashamed about being a coward, so mad at myself that I stood in the same spot, like I was planted there, for what seemed like an hour, hoping that Ted would come back but that never happened. My big chance was over, and I'd failed.

If I'd really met him, shook his hand and gotten his autograph I might have been interviewed on a TV show or had my picture in the paper or been given free tickets to another game or been invited to have a catch with Ted. Who knew? There were so many possibilities if only I hadn't been such a chicken. My father used to say to me, 'You've got to strike while the iron is hot.' Instead, it seemed that all I ever did was strike out at important times like that.

Chapter Nine

Boston's finest

I was standing on the infield grass near home plate when a tall Boston cop came up the dugout steps carrying his police hat in his left hand. He had wavy black hair, a white uniform shirt dark blue trousers and black shoes. My father said once that Boston cops were known as 'Boston's Finest' but I never knew why. All I knew was that he pointed his right index finger at me. He had a somewhat large nose, but his eyes were so happy that I didn't pay much attention to his nose. His ears were somewhat large too, but all-in-all he was a nice-looking guy.

When he pointed at me, I thought I was going to get arrested for trespassing! But when he reached me, he put out his right hand, shook mine and introduced himself as Lou somebody. I think he said Pucillo, but I didn't have any idea about how to spell it. His hand was big and strong when he shook mine and he wanted to know if I needed a ride somewhere. By then, I was already terrified that I might never find my way home, so whatever answer I blurted out must have sounded like a foreign language.

Lou smiled, gave me a nod of his head and told me everything would be okay. He acted as though he knew that I was lost but was trying not to embarrass me, He said to follow him, and we went into the Red Sox dugout and down some stairs into a corridor that was connected to the back of it. Imagine me seeing the inside of the Sox dugout, although I couldn't believe what a mess it was. The players had left Dixie cups, Coke bottles, cellophane candy wrappers, peanut shells, cigarette butts and chewing tobacco spit everywhere in the dugout. It was such a mess that it looked like Mike Dolan's kitchen. Mike was my best friend, and his house was on the opposite corner of Dickens and Havilend Streets from mine. It was the messiest place I'd ever seen before I saw the Sox dugout. If only I'd brought my mother's Kodak Brownie camera so I could prove I'd been there.

I walked behind Lou in silence until we emerged through a doorway into a parking lot outside the ballpark. It only took a few minutes. I thought we might be near the spot where the bus had been parked but if we were, the bus was long gone. Lou said he was off-duty and asked me again if I needed a ride. I told him I'd probably take a streetcar or a subway to get to Ashmont Station; from there I could catch a bus to Wollaston Beach, but the problem was I didn't have any money. To tell you the truth, I didn't know how to even get to any of those places from Fenway Park. Lou laughed and led me to his car, a robin's egg blue Cadillac. It looked pretty new and made me wonder how a cop could afford a Cadillac. I was surprised that Lou put his hand on my shoulder as we were walking toward the car, like we were buddies. My own father had never done that and, I have to admit, Lou made me feel special.

I was also surprised to see a dog, a miniature

French Poodle, jumping around inside the car. Lou had left the windows open just enough for the little gray curly-haired dog to get a breath of fresh air. Lou called the curly dog by the name Koko, and he told me the dog understood foreign languages. I wasn't about to believe that one until Lou opened the driver's door, pointed at the dog and said, 'Ciao, dietro.' Lou cupped his right hand to my left ear and whispered, 'That means 'get in the back' in Italian.' The next thing I knew, Koko jumped over the back of the front seat, turned around and perched himself on the back seat. Lou said Italian was one of seven languages that the dog understood. I have to admit I was dumbfounded. I knew it had to be a trick, but I had no clue how he had taught the dog to understand Italian or any other foreign language.

I admitted that I'd never heard of a French Poodle that understood Italian. Laughing at my gullibility, Lou told me that he'd trained the dog to jump into the back seat whenever he pointed at him, even if he didn't say anything! I thought that was pretty funny and I couldn't believe that I believed any part of Lou's story about a dog understanding seven foreign languages. Bugs Bunny had a saying about a gullible person – 'What a maroon!' That was me sometimes. I should have known there was no such thing as a linguistic dog!

When I told Lou how much trouble I'd be in when I got home and that my parents might have me committed to a mental hospital, the guy felt sorry for me and, after making a call on a nearby pay phone, drove me all the way to Wollaston Beach even though he'd told me that he lived somewhere in Boston. The trip took about forty-five minutes because of rush hour traffic and once we started, Koko jumped into the front and sat between us. I was amused that a tough-looking guy like Lou, a Boston cop, would have such a feminine little dog. I had seen similar dogs with bows and ribbons tied around their ears. His excuse was that it belonged to his girlfriend, and he was taking care of it for the day because she was working somewhere as a waitress, somewhere near a hospital called the Brigham.

When we got to my parents' house, Lou and I came up the front flagstone walk as my parents appeared in the doorway, my father smoking a cigarette, as usual, and my mother with her arms folded across her chest like teachers and nuns used to do when they were getting ready to yell at me. I was cursing myself for getting lost again; no wonder my father thought I was a dope. There I was being brought home by a cop again like a time I tried walking the railroad tracks in Park Ridge. And I was shaking in my boots again. But Lou rose to the occasion, big time, and, as far as I was concerned, kept me from being sent to a loony bin.

I had no idea what he was going to say to my parents but after I heard the words come out of his mouth, I thought that he might be my guardian angel. Lou started by saying, 'Folks, you should be very proud because your son was a real hero today.' He told them a story about how I'd stopped to help an old lady with white hair and a cane who'd fallen off a concrete step at the ballpark and hit her head on a metal railing. I was as flabbergasted by the story as my parents were. Lou continued telling them how I'd become separated from my classmates in the excitement but refused to leave the woman's side until help arrived. Boy, what a pile of crap that was and was I ever embarrassed but Lou remained as cool as a cucumber.

What threw me for a loop was that my mother wasn't screaming at me about getting lost or missing the bus! I couldn't believe that she rode the bus back to Wollaston without knowing where I was. There had to be more to the story but who knew what? My mother could have been a secret agent – I never knew what to expect from her.

Lou even made up some malarkey about how I held the woman's hand and wiped blood from her forehead until a doctor got there and how a newspaper photographer from The Boston Globe had taken my picture using a large square camera with a flash bulb as big as a forty-watt light bulb. He told them that I might be getting an award from the mayor of Boston or from Mr. Yawkey, the Red Sox owner, because of my heroic actions.

I'd never seen anyone put one over on my father before, but I wasn't convinced that my father was buying all of Lou's fictional explanation either. The only reason I thought that my father might have been fooled was because Lou was a uniformed cop, one of Boston's finest, and I'd heard once that my father's father had been a cop in New York City after coming here from Ireland. Maybe that made my father more inclined to believe Lou… maybe.

My mother, on the other hand, looked like she'd been bedazzled by Lou, like he was a matinee idol, and she was a teenage drama queen. I heard her say to my father that Lou was very handsome in his police uniform. That surprised me because my mother was slow to give compliments, especially to non-Irish people and Lou looked Italian and I was pretty sure his name was Italian. As predictable as my parents were, I'd have never guessed that they wouldn't be yelling at me about getting lost. But, as Lou was leaving, my mother thanked him for having called my father from Fenway Park to inform him that I was safe, and that he was going to drive me home. That solved the mystery about why my parents weren't upset.

When Lou shook my hand before getting back into the Cadillac, he winked at me, and we both smiled. I couldn't help noticing that he winked with his right eyelid because I could only wink with my left one. I realized that I'd witnessed what my mother referred to as a 'white lie,' which she'd once said was okay if it did more good than harm. Lou pointed at Koko, the dog jumped into the back seat and off they went.

Chapter Ten

Childhood dreams

I dreamed a lot when I was a kid although I'd prefer to have skipped the childhood dreams because most of them included my mother. And most of those would have to be categorized as nightmares. I definitely preferred dreams about the joys of victory, not the ones about the agonies of defeat. Unfortunately, as a kid I was frequently defeated by my mother's schemes and her low opinion of me. Knowing how dangerous my circumstances were at home, it's a wonder I didn't wind up in jail, or in a prisoner of war camp. But as I've been told, I apparently developed a high level of resilience that can only be explained by the experiences I was forced to endure.

So, let me explain one of many of the ridiculous things that happened in my childhood. This event should shed some light on why I was the black sheep of the family and why my mother and I were operating on different wavelengths for the first ten years of my life and even more years as things turned out.

I was nearly five years old when I went to my first social event. It was at Jimmy Lytel's house. We were living in Park Ridge at that time. To begin with, I didn't like Jimmy Lytel, not even a little and I didn't want to go to his birthday party. I was forced by my mother to attend, then forced by his mother to leave, then forced by my mother to return, then forced by his mother to leave again, then punished by my mother for not bringing home the birthday present I gave Jimmy Lytel at her insistence. I learned what it was like to be one of those hollow white ping pong balls that get smacked back and forth.

Although Jimmy Lytel's party wasn't the first defeat I suffered at the hands of my mother, it best typifies how screwy my mother could be. Jimmy Lytel was this annoying kid who lived in our neighborhood in Park

Ridge, fifteen miles Northwest of Chicago's Downtown Loop. That was the second place we lived near Chicago. The first was a house in Niles, where we stayed only until the wallpaper peeled off the walls in the bedroom shared by my sisters. Reportedly, that event made so much noise in the middle of the night that my sisters were freaked out, believing the house was haunted by a ghost and were too terrified to stay there. Soon after that we moved to Park Ridge.

My family lived in the Chicago area for about four years, starting in the summer of 1942. In the summer of 1946, we would move back to the Boston area. At the time I thought it was partly because of the trouble I got into, and there was plenty of it.

My father sometimes said my picture was on a bulletin board at the Park Ridge post office under a headline that read, 'Wanted Dead or Alive.' He said it was the picture of me wearing a sailor suit that my mother had a photographer take in a department store. I never looked to see if it was really there, but I remember the picture well because it was so embarrassing. If you saw that picture, you'd immediately know that I was innocent of whatever crime I'd been accused, because I looked like a sissy who would never dare to do anything wrong.

So, I'll share a handful of the problems that developed before we left Illinois, starting with the birthday party, and let you make up your own mind about whether I was a troublemaker or an innocent victim. Hopefully, it will give you a better idea of what I was dealing with at the time and what it was like to live with Adelaide Murphy, the woman who told people she was my mother.

I could tell that Jimmy Lytel was a spoiled brat even though I hardly knew him, and hardly knowing him was just fine with me. The day of the party was a warm, sunny Saturday and around noontime, my mother said to me, 'Okay, mister, march yourself upstairs and take a bath.' That annoyed me because, in our house, my bath time was just before bed on Saturday night. I wanted to know what was going on because the noonday bath was going to mess up my plans for the rest of the day, not that I remember now what they were. My mother told me I was going to a birthday party... whether I liked it or not.

I was also annoyed that I hadn't heard about the party earlier. And why was it important to her that I go to someone else's party when I'd never had one of my own? I asked why nobody had told me and my mother said, 'Because Jimmy Lytel's mother didn't invite you, but I heard about it anyway and if she thinks she's going to get away with that, she's got another think coming. Nobody's going to discriminate against any son of mine just because we're Catholics.'

I had no clue what she was talking about but, personally, I'd have been okay with missing the party since I didn't like Jimmy Lytel in the first place. My father, when he overheard the discussion, went bonkers and yelled at my mother, 'What the hell is wrong with you? You've totally lost your marbles! If some dizzy dame doesn't want the kid to go to her party, why the hell do you care? Forget about the damn party, let the kid do what he wants and shut-up about it so I can finish reading the paper.'

That was one of the few times I thought my father was on my side. The others would be when he bought me a bike when I finished 3rd grade, when he took me to the circus during the 4th grade, when he bought me a set of electric trains for Christmas when I was in the 5th grade and when he bought me an aquarium when I was in the 6th grade. Typically, he took my mother's side on every issue no matter what I wanted, and I never thought he liked me much. Instead, I thought he tolerated me and now and then broke down and did something nice. Don't get me wrong; I was thankful for the good times. When he told my mother off about Jimmy Lytel's party, under my breath I said something like, 'Way to go, Dad!' My mother ignored him as usual and dragged me up the stairs toward the bathtub.

There were so many low points in my early life that it's hard to pick just one to illustrate how screwy my relationship with my mother could get but the birthday party will do for a starter, even though I'll have worse things to say about other events later... much worse! But whenever my mother made me put on clean clothes on a Saturday it meant something unpleasant was about to happen and here's how it happened that time.

While I took the bath, she polished my school shoes and after I dried myself off, she combed my hair the way she liked it – the way old geezers parted their hair to cover their bald spots. It looked like something my father called 'a comb-over'. I wasn't bald but the end result looked the same and my hair was so wet that it practically stuck to my scalp. Actually, that's the way it looked in the sailor suit picture.

When she dressed me in a button-up, short-sleeve white shirt, she said I looked handsome, but I didn't give a crap about that stuff. What I cared about was that she didn't make me wear short pants again because that was the pet of all my peeves. I absolutely hated short pants. When she showed me the ones she had selected, I wanted to call her the worst names I could think of because she knew darn well how much I hated short pants. The other kids in the neighborhood wore long pants only – corduroys in the winter and dungarees in the summer. But my mother didn't care about anything except getting what she wanted. She liked me to wear short pants, so I'd look, in her words, like 'a little gentleman instead of a hoodlum.'

For church, she'd sometimes dress me in short pants, white shirt, tie, suit coat and fedora hat, a smaller version of the one my father wore to work every day. If it was cold out, she'd make me wear an overcoat like my father's, but the short pants would still be part of the get-up, whether the weather was hot, cold, wet or dry. And the short pants were held-up by suspenders. Those outfits were nearly as ridiculous looking as the sailor suit. She put the goofy sailor suit picture in a brass frame and displayed it on the Zenith console radio in our living room so everybody could look at it and laugh. Who ever heard of a four-year-old sailor with a white handkerchief dangling out of his breast pocket?

On the day of the party, my mother wanted me to wear the nastiest piece of clothing she'd ever bought for me – a navy-blue French beret! This was a new low, even for her. I quickly tossed the beret into our clothes hamper inside the bath towel I'd used. My mother finally gave-up searching for the silly-looking thing. Oh, she suspected I'd hidden it somewhere, but the party was already starting, and we had to go before she could find it.

I promised myself that I would find a way to burn the beret or pretend that someone stole it. A few days later, it went up in flames when I flipped it into a grass fire in an open field in our neighborhood. It wasn't any coincidence, either. I'm the one who set the grass on fire. Every kid has his limits and I'd have run away from home before wearing a beret. Anyway, my mother and I had developed a confrontational relationship before I ever knew what the word meant. She was the most annoying person I knew.

My sisters and brother would have agreed regarding the beret, but they, like me, were afraid to say anything that might make my mother mad. That was like poking a stick into a nest of rattlesnakes. My mother's favorite saying was, 'Children should be seen and not heard,' and that's how life was in our house. If the kids wanted to avoid trouble, we had to follow orders and keep our mouths shut unless we were asked a direct question.

When I was young, I never knew what was wrong with my mother. I concluded that there must have been something wrong with me. Hard as I tried, nothing I did ever seemed to be good enough for her. I think kids are inclined to accept their parents' behavior until something happens that's so dramatically wrong it can't be ignored any longer. Jimmy Lytel's birthday party was just such a turnaround event for me.

My mother asked me which of my illustrated books was my favorite. I told her it was the red and tan one about Mickey Mouse. She wrapped it in gift paper, sealed it with Scotch tape and said we were going to bring it to the party as a gift for Jimmy Lytel. I felt like my mother had just hit me with a gut punch. She was going to give my favorite picture book to a kid I didn't like. A kid I hardly knew. A kid who didn't invite me to his birthday party even though I lived just around the corner.

What was wrong with my mother anyway? This time it couldn't have been my fault again, or could it? Look, I had lots of better things to do on a Saturday. Even drinking curdled milk would have been better than going to Jimmy Lytel's party. But what I wanted never seemed to matter much to my mother. Things were always her way or no way.

So, off we went to the Lytel's house. I remember it well because it was a warm, sunny day without a cloud in the sky and we saw a silver airplane, flying low, heading to O'Hare Airport. O'Hare was in the next town, Des Plains, which used to confuse me because I thought the town was named Des 'Planes' because it had an airport. The pleasant weather prompted my mother to say, 'This must be what it's like in heaven, but I doubt if you'll ever find out.' When I was a kid, I used to hear that kind of mean comment a lot. What the heck, I was trying really hard to be liked even though it hadn't worked yet, and as things would turn out, it wasn't about to work anytime soon, either.

Most of the houses in our neighborhood were covered with cinnamon-color brick but Jimmy Lytel's house had tan and gray fieldstone on the front and brown wooden clapboards everywhere else. When we walked around the corner from South Greenwood Avenue, my mother dragged me to the Lytel's front walk, sent me up the stairs to ring the doorbell, and then walked back home.

The house had a red front door with a rounded top that reminded me of a drawing I'd seen of the cottage in the forest where the seven dwarfs were supposed to live. Mrs. Lytel, a thin woman with frizzy, reddish-brown hair, pasty make-up and way too much bright-red lipstick, answered the door. I told her my name and asked if I could go to the party. Boy, was that ever embarrassing. She asked my name, took my gift and led me toward the dining room where the celebration was taking place.

Jimmy was a small kid with sandy brown hair who seemed to whine about everything. He was one of those hands-in-his-pockets kids that I'd been told by my mother not to be. When I walked into his dining room, I thought the kid had a tattoo on his left arm until I realized it was colored frosting – green, pink, blue and white – from a birthday cake. I never knew much about birthday cakes. I couldn't remember ever getting one.

Then his mother asked Jimmy why I hadn't been invited, and the little creep told her that he didn't like me and nobody else did either. What the heck? We had just moved there, and I hadn't even met most of the kids. Everyone heard him say it and I was absolutely crushed, like a grand piano had been dropped on my head, although I thought those pianos were called Grant pianos after a Civil War general.

While I waited, frozen in my tracks, his mother asked him if it would be okay if I stayed anyway. But he told her nobody wanted me there and he pitched a fit about it. His mother said I'd have to leave, which was okay with me even though I knew it was going to infuriate my mother. Jimmy's mother ushered me out the front door with a firm push on my tush, telling me not to let the door hit me on the way.

When I got home, my mother went wild, and I thought she was going to break my right arm off and whack me over the head with it. If she had, I'd have looked like the one-arm mannequin in the Sears Roebuck clothing department, the one my brother Jimmy called 'Lefty.' She ordered me to go back to the party and get my gift back, like I hadn't already had enough shame for one day. I obeyed and when Mrs. Lytel let me inside the front door, I asked her to return the gift, but she refused. She said it wasn't polite to ask people to return presents and said people who did were called 'Indian givers.' I thought that was a pretty stupid thing to say and didn't even get what she meant.

After I told her that my mother was going to kill me if I didn't bring the book home, she pushed me backward, through the front door opening and then closed the door in my face. It came so close that it practically smacked me in the nose. When I got home and told my mother what happened, it infuriated her, and I was the one who got punished. I was sent up to my bedroom for the rest of the day for being, according to her, 'a little sissy.'

Chapter Eleven

Protestants

From that day forward, the only kid in the neighborhood that I played with regularly was Larry Blewis, who had been adopted by a family named Hesse, who lived diagonally across the alley from our house. In retrospect, it was the start of a pattern where I gravitated toward people who were confused like me, and Larry was definitely one of them.

My mother had warned me that the people in Larry's family were Protestants so I should be very careful that I didn't get too friendly with them because his family might try to convert me, whatever that meant. She also told me that Larry wasn't quite right in the head so I should leave immediately if he started doing anything weird like touching himself, 'you know where,' although I didn't know where.

There were lots of times when I didn't have the slightest notion of what my mother was talking about. Actually, I thought Larry was okay. It was his mother who I thought was weird. Helen Hesse had long, blondish-brown hair, large brown eyes, didn't smile much, and when she did, sometimes I'd see lipstick smudged on her teeth, the teeth my father said looked like the wooden 'choppers' that George Washington wore. Mrs. Hesse had the longest ear lobes I'd ever seen, kind of like a bloodhound, and for some reason she made me uncomfortable whenever she touched me, like she was the wicked witch who flew around on a broomstick.

Mrs. Hesse was the skinniest woman I'd ever seen. The blood vessels in her hands and arms looked like there were blue worms under her skin. She and my father had one thing in common – they were what my mother called 'chain smokers,' and their cigarette smoke was irritating enough to gag people, especially me. If I was looking for my father inside our house, my mother would usually say, 'Look for the room with all the smoke.' Obviously, my mother didn't approve of smoking.

It wasn't long before I decided that I might have been adopted, too, because it seemed like Larry's family treated him with the same coolness that I got from mine. Neither of our families seemed to hug or kiss at all. If I was adopted, it might have explained a lot about why sometimes my mother wasn't very nice to me. It also could have explained why my older brother and two older sisters didn't seem to like me much – because I was adopted or a stepchild or something else that was abnormal. There was nothing I could do about any of that other than accept my circumstances.

My circle of friends was pretty small – just Larry

Blewis, me and Bobo, my Teddy bear and my best friend, even though he was only two feet high when sitting and couldn't walk or talk. That was okay with me because I was sure that he liked me as much as I liked him. His back, arms and legs were dark brown fur. He had soft, tan fur everywhere else except his tummy, which had white fur. His face had brown and white button eyes and the tip of his tiny red tongue was just barely visible below his nose. Our friendship got me through a lot of tough times when I didn't think anyone else cared about me. I may not have known what it meant to be an outcast, but I knew how it felt to be one. And I continued to feel that way until I was ten years old and got lost at Fenway Park.

To this day, I still remember how lost I sometimes felt when we lived in Park Ridge. When the sun had set on warm nights, I'd sometimes lie back on the redwood lawn furniture in our side yard looking up at the stars. I had a spooky but realistic sense about having come from up there somewhere. Not in heaven exactly, but somewhere among the stars. I don't know where I got that idea or how I thought I'd gotten from up there to down here but that was just the belief I had. I used to wonder if I'd be going back there some day. Looking back, that all seems pretty dopey now, but it was my reality when I was little.

Anyway, that's an example of how life usually was between me and my family circle, especially Adelaide Murphy. One time she said her middle name was Healey, which turned out to be her maiden name. Another time my older sister, Dorothy, told me that my mother used to have another last name beginning with the letter W, whatever that meant. As a kid, I wasn't sure about who and what she really was, mostly whether or not she really was my mother or had adopted me.

I always sensed that I really wasn't part of the family and feared that my mother might send me back to wherever I came from. My sister, Dorothy, who was two years older than Jimmy, four older than Barbara and thirteen older than me, once told me that I belonged to a different mother because the hospital in Boston, where I'd been born, had accidently switched me with another baby. The rest of Dorothy's story was that my mother was trying to prove that I wasn't her kid and, when she did, she was going to send me back to Boston. That was pretty scary to me, so I tried not to think about it much. At the time, I never mentioned it to anyone except Bobo. I knew that he'd understand.

Of course, there were lots of times when my mother was nice to me. She once answered one of my questions, but that was an exception. Most of my questions were just plain ignored. The first question I remember her ever answering was why there was a framed picture of her in an evening gown on the dresser in her bedroom. She told me that it was taken when she was a 'high fashion' clothing model in Boston, before she married my father. Dorothy told me that it was true that my mother was once a model because she had something called a 'peaches and cream complexion,' which for models was supposed to be a good quality. Not knowing much about those things, I

believed her. At that time of my life, I didn't know much about anything.

I always thought my mother had a really nice smile, although I didn't see it often and her blue-gray eyes seemed to glow when the light was just right. My mother had brown hair at times and at other times it was blond. I thought she was prettier as a blond. She had a narrow nose that she said was a good thing and an important part of being beautiful. She used to pull on my nose so it wouldn't get too wide. I began to fear that I was going to look like Pinocchio from all that nose pulling. That was only one of the nutty things she did, and I had to promise to keep pulling my nose when she wasn't around to do it.

Although she answered the evening gown question, there was a question I asked at a later time that made her so mad I thought she might bite my head off. I had been snooping around inside her hope chest where she kept hundreds of photographs – of her, her family and some friends. What caught my attention was that many of the pictures contained someone without a head. It was some guy wearing a bathing suit in most of the pictures. It was one of those old-time bathing suits that had a tank top and a bottom that went down to his knees.

Someone had cut up the photos so that the guy was missing his head. When I asked what happened to it, my mother went ballistic, slamming the lid on my arm. She screamed at me to never go into her bedroom again and to never look at anything in the hope chest or in her dresser, or anything else belonging to her. I wondered who could have been so bad that she cut his head off, but I never got an answer from her or from my siblings. I gave up the questioning.

My mother was wearing a bathing suit in some of the pictures with the headless guy. She had a curvy figure, like some of the movie actresses I'd seen on posters. All-in-all, I recall her being very attractive when she got dressed up and she could pick out fabulous, large hats to wear. People used to compliment her hats all the time. I believed that she had been a model just by looking at her hats, clothes and makeup. She definitely knew how to wear nice things. I once heard a woman who was visiting us say that my mother was stunning when she got dressed up to go out. I never heard my father say anything about her being stunning, attractive or even looking nice, but he never seemed to compliment anyone.

The story that my sister, Barbara, used to tell me was that I was an orphan and had been sent to my parents on a train together with our dog, a pointer puppy, who was six weeks old at the time. Supposedly, my mother's oldest sister, Katie, was a nun at a school for orphans in Kansas, and that I had been smuggled onto the baggage car of the train and kept in a cage like the one that the puppy was in. Later, Barbara denied ever saying it. Maybe that was just my imagination.

Supposedly, the dog and I were both on trial to see if my family wanted to keep us, and that either of us could get sent back to Katie if we caused too much trouble. Barbara said that she only wanted to keep the puppy and I believed her even though she later said that she was kidding. Barbara was always quick to embarrass me about something or other. I always wanted her to like me, but my efforts were wasted. It was impossible for me to figure out why my family disliked me, but it was what it was. Barbara was nice most of the time and, in later years, I concluded that my mother didn't treat her any better than me.

Dorothy looked old enough to be my mother and like a grown woman. By the time I was five, Dorothy was working as a telephone operator in Park Ridge and didn't spend as much time at home as my other two siblings. Dorothy was very pretty and had a curvy figure like my mother. But my mother warned me that Dorothy couldn't be trusted, not to let her get too cozy with me and not to believe anything she told me. My mother sometimes called Dorothy 'light-fingered Louie' and told me she had to be watched carefully or she'd steal everything that wasn't nailed down. What kind of a thing was that to tell me about my sister? It made me wonder what the heck she was telling other people about me.

Barbara didn't look at all like Dorothy. She looked much younger and more like a typical teenage girl than a movie actress but was nevertheless attractive. Barbara was thin, athletic and very sensitive. My mother once said, 'That one will cry at the drop of a hat.'

What I remember is how easily Barbara got mad and how she hated me going into the bedroom she shared with Dorothy. Whenever I tried to go in there, I'd get the door slammed shut in my face. I tried hard to get along with Barbara, but it would become a lifetime chore. To her, I was 'the little monster,' especially when our parents made her babysit for me.

Although Dorothy dressed in fancier clothes, Barbara was more comfortable in jeans, saddle shoes and pigtails. I felt sorry for her because my mother and father criticized her so much. They'd just keep picking on her until the tears started and she'd run into her bedroom and cry hysterically. Then one of them would order her to stop crying, 'or else.' It never seemed fair to me. But who was I to be feeling sorry for anyone else? I got criticized plenty myself. Of course, they criticized Dorothy too, but she wasn't nearly as sensitive about it as Barbara. It didn't seem like Jimmy got criticized as much as the girls, and I assumed it was because he had a hare lip and cleft palate and my parents cut him some slack. I would learn later that in our family nobody got any slack.

As to my father, my mother used to tell me to keep away from him unless he wanted to talk to me. She explained that he had a drinking problem, which made him angry most of the time and it was better to stay away from him whenever possible. She told me that he had smashed their car, a two-tone, brown and tan Oldsmobile, into a stone wall next to a dairy farm in Milton once when he was drunk. My mother's head went through the windshield and required 12 stitches in the middle of her forehead to close the wound. The scar was visible for the rest of her life. The accident also broke one of her hips, which required surgery and several months of recuperation. No wonder she criticized my father's driving so often. According to her, he had almost killed her in the accident at the dairy farm which may have been the truth.

Chapter Twelve

Jimmy Wah-wah

Just as my sisters were roommates, my brother Jimmy and I were roommates. Dorothy told me once that some kids at Jimmy's school called him Jimmy Wah-Wah because he had a speech impediment. Jimmy and I shared bunk beds, me on the bottom. In addition to being my brother and my roommate, I always hoped he'd become my best friend, but that would never happen. Anyway, my Teddy bear, Bobo was always there for me.

The simplest explanation was that Jimmy never wanted to spend any time with me because I was usually pestering him about something or other, and because he was eleven years older, he didn't want to do the things I enjoyed. Once, when Jimmy wasn't home, I tried using the homemade radio he had built from a kit with a soldering iron. When he found out I had broken one of the copper wires and the radio didn't work, he choked me pretty hard. I was four and Jimmy was fifteen at the time and we didn't have much in common.

But we did sleep in the same bunk bed, which was scary because he had a problem with bed wetting, and he slept above me. I used to worry about getting peed on at night although I never did. My mother would freak out some mornings and scream her head off at Jimmy. He'd usually hang his head in shame and cry. I'd usually cry too. I must have loved my brother because I cried for him a lot.

My mother told me to stay away from Jimmy because of his physical deformities – the harelip, cleft palate and speech impediment. And according to her, Jimmy needed special attention. I didn't know exactly what that meant, but I did as I was told.

It was weird living with Dorothy, Barbara and Jimmy and not being close or even friendly with any of them. They often hung around together, and I was always an outsider. It was pretty much the same with my parents. I felt like an outsider with them too. Most of my conversations with my parents happened when one of them wanted to criticize me for having done something wrong or not having done something right. Usually, it was my mother.

There was no denying that Jimmy's facial deformity was severe, as was his speech difficulty. When Jimmy spoke, his speech had a nasal tone like his nose was stuffed up from a serious head cold. It definitely was difficult to understand some of his words, which was why kids at school nicknamed him Jimmy Wah-Wah. That was about the cruelest thing I ever heard, and it made my sister Barbara furious. I can remember her crying about it and screaming about hating the kids that mocked him. She wanted to beat them up and probably could have. So did I, but I was, in Jimmy's words, 'a little pipsqueak.' Plus, I'm pretty sure I never looked very tough in the sissy clothes my mother kept forcing me to wear, especially short pants.

In spite of his handicaps, my brother had more talent than the rest of us by far, more than all of us put together. Jimmy was the best artist I'd ever seen. His ability to draw pictures, especially cartoons, amazed me. He could produce his own episodes of the newspaper cartoons and do them freehand and in color. He could play popular songs on his harmonica. His music sounded like it came from some country music station. It amazed me that he could play a harmonica at all because of his mouth deformity. But he played it well, better than I could, that's for sure.

And baseball? He could throw a baseball as fast as a bullet and catch a fly ball or a grounder flawlessly. I'd try to follow him to the baseball field because I loved watching him, but he'd throw rocks at me to keep me from getting too close to him. And then there was hockey. I couldn't imagine anyone skating faster than Jimmy. He reminded me of one of those superhero characters in comic books. Dorothy and Barbara were good skaters too but watching Jimmy zip across the ice, was like those movie theater newsreels of race cars flying around an oval track. It looked to me like he could skate backward just as fast as forward.

But of all the things Jimmy enjoyed, shooting targets with his Red Ryder BB rifle was the coolest. I'd sneak down the alley next to our garage in Park Ridge to watch him shooting at empty tin cans. I was always trying to figure out how I could get my hands on that rifle so I could shoot it without getting caught by Jimmy or my father.

In spite of my parents insistence that Jimmy keep the rifle on the top shelf of our bedroom closet where I couldn't possibly reach it, Jimmy accidentally left it on his bunk one afternoon shortly before I started kindergarten. I saw it there the moment Jimmy left the room and made sure not to remind him to put it away. I climbed the ladder to his bed and took the rifle to the top landing of the stairs that led down to the front door of our house. As luck would have it, my sisters were standing at the open front door chatting with one of their friends, Carolyn Wolfe, who lived around the corner on South Chester Avenue.

I had no idea that the rifle was cocked and loaded. All I knew was I'd seen a cowboy movie where some cowhand was lying on the ground and shooting a rifle. So, I tried lying on the floor at the top of the stairs and aimed the sight on the rifle between Carolyn's eyes. While I pretended I was shooting Carolyn, I accidently did shoot her, and boy, did she scream! I was so scared that I wanted to run away from home before my parents found out what I had done. All I did was pull the trigger and the rifle butt hit me in the shoulder as the BB struck her in the throat. I saw the blood come out. While my sisters were hollering at me at the top of their lungs, Carolyn ran home screaming loud enough for the whole neighborhood to hear her. Good thing I had lousy aim, or I might have shot her eye out!

It wasn't long before the Park Ridge police arrived, just as my parents were getting home from wherever they had been. The black and white police car had a twirling red light on the roof and there were two policeman and a third man, Carolyn's father. Some of the neighbors – the nosey ones – came out of their houses to watch the commotion. The cops asked me all kinds of questions and my parents had to agree to take the rifle away from Jimmy.

If Jimmy didn't hate me before that, he definitely hated me afterward. Jimmy's comment at the crime scene was, 'I'll get even with you for this, you little asshole!' That was the first time he ever swore at me, and it wouldn't be the last. All I knew was that I had so many feelings for Jimmy that I could never have called him nasty names or sworn at him. Never!

Finally, the police and Mr. Wolfe left. I don't know what they decided except that Jimmy's rifle was gone. I remember my father saying something to me like, 'You had to shoot someone who's father's a lawyer? How stupid could you be? Next time you want to start trouble, pick someone who's father's a janitor.'

My mother? Her comment, as usual, was, 'I just don't know what's wrong with you? You'll be the death of me yet.' I was always getting blamed for stuff that I never meant to do. And the more I tried to stay out of trouble, the more I got into trouble.

Jimmy was definitely out to get even with me after the BB episode, even more than usual. Jimmy and my two sisters were always looking for ways to antagonize and scare me. Locking me in the garage was high up on their list of favorites, and so was locking me outside the house, in my underpants, on one of our two deck porches, especially in the winter. After the shooting incident, Jimmy found the perfect way to get even with me. One day while my parents went shopping, he locked me in our basement laundry room, which had no windows, no inside light switch, and no inside door lock. Once locked inside the pitch-black room, it was like I was in solitary confinement.

There was a tin laundry chute from the two upper floors of the house that opened into the laundry room and made the place sound like an echo chamber. After locking the door, Barbara and Jimmy raced upstairs, one to each floor. They opened the sliding panels to the chute and hollered spooky threats into it, saying they were boogeymen who were about to slide down the chute to get me. Dorothy stayed in the basement to rattle the doorknob to the room, pretending she was a vampire coming in to bite my neck and drink my blood.

It must have been my blood-curdling screams or pounding my fists on the walls or kicking the crap out of the door that saved me. When they let me out, I thought they were going to die laughing, especially my brother. Fortunately, as I'd get older, bigger and smarter, the three of them would lose interest in harassing me, which was okay by me.

But it wasn't just daytime horrors that troubled me. Nighttime could be really scary when my father came home after stopping at a place called Bonnie's Tavern in Des Plains. According to my mother, this was part of his drinking problem. I didn't know much about it except that I'd try to be asleep before he came home because there was no way of telling what would happen when he was drunk. Once, in the middle of the night, my father parked his car in our neighbors' front shrubbery, in front of the bay window at their dining room, mistaking it for our garage. The next morning the Park Ridge Police were at our house again, trying to get answers about how our car got into their shrubs and who was going to pay for the damage.

My father would often have violent arguments with my mother, usually causing her to kick him out of the bedroom. When that happened, my father would come into my room and sleep with me and Bobo, which scared us a lot. James Augustine Murphy was not an easy man to deal with because of his anger and his size. When he would fall into my bed, there was hardly any room for me and Bobo. I usually got pinned against a wall and couldn't move until morning. My father was a hair under six feet, two inches and slightly less than 240 pounds. Some people called him 'Big Jim Murphy.' He was definitely an imposing figure of a man. He had arms like a lumberjack, a barrel chest and, compared with my mother, was a foot taller and 100 pounds heavier.

I knew very little about him and his family. He had a sister named Dot who came to stay with us for a week every summer. I once overheard my Aunt Dot telling my mother that her mother had a child called Annie who died in a fall from a third floor deck while her mother was hanging out laundry. Annie was resting in an infant's seat on a railing when her mother accidentally backed into the seat and Annie died upon impact with the ground.

She also said that their family had lived in an unheated tenement building in Greenwich Village and the only way they could bathe and cook was for my father and his older brother, John, to walk through the lower Manhattan train yards and fill their pockets with lumps of coal for their stove. They called it shopping but the railroad police called it stealing.

I had also heard that my father quit school after the 8th grade to help support his mother and three sisters because his father, a New York City cop, died from throat cancer at the early age of forty-four. According to Aunt Dot, my father worked as a butcher's assistant days, which included unloading meat wagons and carrying sides of beef up a ladder to a storage loft. He also worked a night job as an inside messenger, delivering telegrams on roller skates at Western Union headquarters in Manhattan, a block-long building with marble floors.

Aunt Dot also told me that my father once ran down a woman who was crossing a street in New York City and dragged her for a block before the police stopped him. I also learned from my sister, Dorothy, that he started going to AA meetings for people with drinking problems about two years after we moved to Park Ridge and the letters 'AA' became a common, positive term in our house for the rest of my father's life. My strongest memory about Jimmy's relationship with my father was that they didn't seem to get along and my father seemed to be angry with Jimmy most of the time, which I never understood but there wasn't anything I could do about it.

Chapter Thirteen

Great Chicago fire

There had been a famous fire in Chicago about seventy years before we moved there. It was frequently referred to as the Great Chicago Fire and there was a myth about it having been started by Mrs. O'Leary's cow kicking over a kerosene lantern in her barn. For some reason, that myth tickled my father and I remember him talking about it more than a few times. I remember a lot of my father's examples of this, that and the other thing. Jim Murphy was known as a great storyteller and my mother said that he was often asked to speak at AA meetings because of that. He was called Jim M by other AA members. He had large hands with freckles like the freckles on his large arms. His head was nearly bald, and he was very fussy about how the few brown hairs he had were arranged. His hat size was extra-large which, according to him, was an indication of extraordinary intelligence, one of his occasional jokes.

That was another thing my mother warned me not to talk about, because my father dropped out of school at the end of the 8th grade and he was embarrassed to tell that to anyone, especially the dentists that he sold equipment to who had at least twelve more years of education than he did. In spite of having little formal education, my father was an avid reader of self-help books, scientific information, philosophy, religion, and medical facts. He was also devoted to doing crossword puzzles, the more difficult the better. Jim Murphy was a person who was more comfortable in a suit and tie, and when dressed-up he looked like someone important, like a bank president. Although having only an 8th grade education, he spoke like an orator and was frequently sought after for public speaking appearances, whether at dental equipment events or AA meetings. He would only buy quality brands of clothing and in the words of my mother, 'Jim Murphy always looked like a million bucks when he got dressed-up.'

When he yelled at someone, it sounded like a bomb exploding. I still clearly remember how he always seemed to be yelling at me the loudest, especially on the occasion of what became known as the Great Chicago Fire at the Murphy house. My brother had gotten a molded cardboard pumpkin for Halloween, the year I started kindergarten at the Roosevelt School. He put it on the chest of drawers in our bedroom. It was colored orange and had been pressed into the shape of a pumpkin head with openings where the eyes, nose and mouth would be. Inside was cellophane, colored to look like the parts of a human face, such as the eyeballs. Attached to the inside bottom was a stubby white candle that could be lighted to make the pumpkin look spooky when the room was dark. Of course, my mother told me to never try lighting the candle. What she actually said was, 'Knowing you, you'll set the room on fire, so I want you to promise me faithfully that you won't light the candle unless Jimmy is in the room.'

Naturally, I promised that I wouldn't, but the temptation for a five-year-old kid was overwhelming. I just wanted to see it light-up once, just once, in the dark, after which I was going to blow it out right away. Well, the problem turned out to be that when I lit a match and turned it upside down to reach the wick of the candle, it burned my fingers and when I dropped the match, the cellophane caught fire and when I blew on the cellophane there was an explosive WHOOSH sound, followed by a slow-motion fireball.

When the smoke cleared, I could see that the whole pumpkin was ablaze as were my mother's two green, yellow and brown plaid curtains behind it. Every time I blew harder, the fire got bigger and when I started waving my pillow at it, the window curtains started burning like crazy and there was black smoke everywhere, especially on the ceiling.

After that, I was known as the kid who started the Great Chicago Fire. Of course, my father called me a damned dope again. Thinking back, that's pretty funny now, but I thought my head was going to explode when my father started yelling at me. It was my sister Barbara who came to the rescue. She was in her bedroom when the fire started spreading and she ran into the bathroom next to the room with the pumpkin. She filled a plastic drinking cup with water and threw it on the fire. I think she actually did it several times. Meanwhile, my mother was running up the stairs yelling, 'The house is on fire, run for your life!'

The pumpkin had disintegrated into a snowstorm of drifting ashes that looked like little gray parachutes floating downward. There was a trail of melted white wax inching its way across the top of the dresser and over the edge. It began to look like a winter icicle hanging off a roof gutter. When Barbara doused the flames, the room was filled with smoke and soot, but you'd have thought she was Wonder Woman that day. I was amazed at how courageous she had been.

Then came the worst part – my father coming home later and examining the damage. He blamed everyone for the fire, but mostly me. The last thing he said to me was, 'What the hell is wrong with you anyway? I just finished painting these goddamn walls and woodwork and you come along and with one match you practically burn the house down. Are you nuts or just plain stupid? I knew you were a dope, but you're even dumber than I thought!' My mother's comment was, 'You're just a little devil and I'll get even with you for this.' It usually seemed that someone was waiting to get even with me for something!

Jimmy had the nerve to gripe about the smell the fire left behind, which was ridiculous since his shoes smelled ten times worse – those things stunk to high heaven! Not only did they stink but he used to shove them under my bed at night, right under my pillow. The smell was bad enough to make a normal person toss his cookies.

As much trouble as I got into, Jimmy ultimately let me off the hook for having caused the loss of his BB rifle. He was, at his core, a gentle person who seemed to tolerate his physical deformities rather well. He had the best sense of humor of anyone I knew, and I loved to hear him laugh. Even when something funny went over my head, listening to Jimmy laugh made me laugh. He seemed to know the day, time and radio station where every comedy show was on the air. He'd sit on the living room floor in front of our Zenith console radio laughing like crazy at some of the humor. I loved it when Jimmy was happy. I thought he deserved it more than anyone else.

And the way he had shaped his Rawlings baseball glove was a creation of art better than any sculpture I'd seen. He called the process 'forming a deep pocket,' which was supposed to make it almost impossible to make an error. His glove could stand up by itself without falling over and he'd always leave a baseball in the pocket to keep the shape he wanted. He said it was called a fielder's glove as opposed to the kinds of gloves that catchers and first basemen used. I loved slipping my hand inside it when Jimmy wasn't home. Just the smell of the leather and the glove oil was as enjoyable as a two-scoop strawberry sundae at the Rexall lunch counter in downtown Park Ridge. To this day I still remember that there were two wire carousels at the far end of that counter, one with action comic books like Superman and the other with stories about classic adventures from literature like Robin Hood.

There were several other events involving my brother, the most important of which, the one that affected me the most as a youngster, was when my father brought Jimmy to Chicago to take a train all by himself to Massachusetts to have reconstructive surgery done on his nose, lip and mouth. I'm pretty sure that happened the summer after I finished 1st grade but don't quote me on it.

This will give you a memorable example of how clueless my parents could be about other people's feelings. One Saturday morning, my father drove Jimmy and me into Chicago to put Jimmy on a train at a humongous building called Union Station. Jimmy was going to visit a doctor who was scheduled to perform surgery and provide speech therapy for two months at a hospital in Holyoke, Massachusetts, about a hundred miles west of Boston. My father got me up, told me to eat some Cheerios and get into the back seat of the car while he put Jimmy's suitcase in the trunk.

My father had decided to send Jimmy to a cleft palate specialist, the one who had earlier performed surgery to close his palate when the family used to live near Boston. To this day I can't figure out why Jimmy had to go a thousand miles from Chicago for surgery to repair the problem. Wouldn't you think that a big city like Chicago would have a skilled surgeon who could have made the correction so that Jimmy could have stayed near home? What I also wondered was why my father waited until Jimmy was practically full grown before scheduling the surgery. I'm guessing that he put it off until Jimmy was about to enter high school, knowing that, without the surgery, Jimmy would probably be mocked at Maine Township High even more than he'd been mocked at the other schools he'd attended.

I was with my father when he left Jimmy on a train below the terminal building, where there were rows and rows of trains waiting for passengers to get on and off. The trains were stopped between steel columns that seemed to be holding up the building. There was a row of concrete platforms between the trains so that huge wooden wagons with steel wheels and spokes, carrying passengers' luggage, could be pulled by a tractor to the correct baggage cars.

A conductor looked at my brother's ticket and led us to the train heading toward Boston. I thought we were getting on the wrong train because, although I could barely read, I figured out that the maroon train cars were painted with the words 'Pennsylvania Railway' in gold on the sides. My father said he was sure it was the right train and found Jimmy a seat at the back of one of the cars. He nonchalantly told Jimmy not to be scared, wished him luck and casually shook his hand. That was about as warm as feelings ran in our family. It was very rare to be hugged or kissed. Most times we shook hands.

When we left Jimmy, I thought he was crying but wasn't sure because my father told me not to look back. I know I was crying; it was the saddest thing I'd ever seen. My big brother was about to spend a day and a night on a train with a bunch of strangers, followed by a couple of months of surgeries, recoveries, speech therapy and who-knew-what else? What kind of parenting was that? I couldn't believe that nobody in our family was going to Massachusetts with Jimmy, or, as far as I knew, even planned on visiting him while he was there. If I'd known earlier, I'd have packed a bag and hidden on the train so Jimmy wouldn't have had to go alone.

It felt to me like he was going off to fight in World War II and I couldn't help wondering if I would ever see him again. Actually, there were so many military people on the train car, especially sailors, that my father said that Jimmy's handicap had a silver lining. It prevented him from being drafted and possibly being killed in the war, which was probably the only good thing about it.

When my father and I walked back toward the station building, I was sadder than I had ever been. It was unusually hot for June and unbearably humid in the train station – my father called the air 'sticky,' but to me it felt like a wet bath towel. On the platform, there were clouds of yellowish smoke that smelled so bad that I was afraid to breathe in. There were bursts of steam coming from the gigantic metal spoke wheels of the engines and the ceiling above the trains kept everything dim, dismal and dreary looking. I'd heard that riding trains was supposed to be fun, but I didn't believe it after going to Union Station to see my brother off on his trip to the Holyoke Hospital for an encounter with a surgeon's knife and a man named Dr. Fitzgibbons.

I was ashamed about the way my parents were treating Jimmy. It seemed as though they didn't understand what he'd be going through. Maybe they didn't, which would have been more shameful. What the heck, even though I was just a little kid, I knew that it wasn't right to treat somebody that way, especially when he was part of our family, not to mention that he was my only brother, my roommate and my next best friend to Bobo, even if he did like to throw rocks at me at times. At least I hoped he was my friend.

It was hard to know those things for sure because, in our family, life was kind of weird – no matter what was going on, everyone was supposed to act like everything was great. If a crisis was brewing, we were supposed to ignore it. If my mother wasn't talking to my father, everyone was supposed to act normal. If my father had been hollering at my mother, sometimes calling her the village idiot, we were supposed to act like nothing happened. My mother wanted us to convince the neighbors that we were the perfect American family. What a joke that was! Looking back, I realize that we were one of the weirdest families ever.

You see, although I wouldn't find out until I was twenty-eight years old, my parents had been married to other people before marrying each other. My mother was married to a man named Norman Wadleigh and Dorothy was her daughter. Jimmy and Barbara were my father's children, born when he was married to a woman named Ida Mahoney. That was why nobody would tell me anything about the past and why my siblings avoided me. That was the 'big secret.' Apparently, my mother had threatened the other three kids with death by public hanging if any of them let the 'cat out of the bag' about the divorces. It wasn't just any secret, it was the big one, punishable by death! It was what caused my family to become America's number one dysfunctional sextet. No wonder I felt like an outsider, an orphan, adopted and alone!

By church rules, my parents had been excommunicated from the Catholic Church because divorce and remarriage were illegal according to Vatican Law. That law prevented divorced people from participating in the sacraments of the church. It was the reason that my parents didn't go to Confession and Communion! Technically, it made me an illegitimate Catholic and my parents didn't want me and other people to know the truth. I only found out by accident when I tripped over the corner of an oriental rug in my mother's bedroom many years later. There, I found divorce papers, a civil marriage license and my birth certificate hidden. Everyone had kept the secret for twenty-eight years... mainly by avoiding me.

After the rest of the family had gone to so much trouble to keep the big secret, I didn't have the heart to tell them that I had learned the truth. It seemed to invalidate their efforts to protect me from feeling unworthy, even though the truth set me free emotionally. What a revolting development that was – I became the final keeper of the big secret that had distorted my life so dramatically. I went from the victim of my parents' secret to the person protecting my parents from their secret. Talk about a 'topsy-turvy' circumstance!

Chapter Fourteen

Railroad Tracks

While living in Park Ridge, one of my mother's rules was that each day was supposed to be a new beginning and yesterday was supposed to be forgotten. On schooldays, my mother would be cooking breakfast, the dog would be out in the side yard next to the alley taking a poop and the kids would be scurrying to get dressed in time for the arrival of the school bus. On weekends, there were chores to be done on Saturday; Sunday meant Mass and catechism classes before everyone gathered back at our house for Sunday dinner. On the outside, our family probably did look like we were ordinary, everyday people, but on the inside, there was enough tension to split the Rock of Gibraltar in two.

I couldn't understand why my mother didn't go to the train station with Jimmy. After I'd seen how Jimmy was treated at the train station by my father, you'd think that I'd have realized what would happen to me if I did anything outrageous, like walking the railroad tracks from Park Ridge to Holyoke. But I didn't think it was outrageous. How was I supposed to know that Holyoke was a thousand miles away? Nobody told me that. I was thinking about helping Jimmy, not about how much trouble I might get into; I was thinking that someone in the family should be with him and why not me?

After all, I didn't have to go to school; it was summer vacation. In fact, I didn't have to do anything important, so early the next morning before anyone else was awake, I headed for the railroad tracks closest to our house with Bobo. I had to keep asking people which direction went to Boston before some skinny lady wearing a red straw hat with yellow make-believe daisies gave me an answer. Once she pointed out the way, off we went.

It wasn't like I hadn't planned ahead; I'd made us peanut butter and jelly sandwiches and put them with a banana and a white paper napkin into a brown lunch bag for the trip. I even took my jacket in case it rained. I never thought that my parents might get scared because I was lost or had been kidnapped or who knows what. I wasn't smart enough to figure all that stuff out.

Five years later, when I'd look back to the railroad tracks fiasco, I understood my mother's reluctance to turn me loose to go to a ball game in Boston but, in my defense, I thought visiting Jimmy was the right thing to do. Even though my intentions were noble, the whole thing ended in disaster when Bobo and I were brought home in the back seat of a black and white police cruiser by two Park Ridge cops who responded to a phone call about some dumb little kid walking in the middle of the rails heading toward Chicago. One of the cops recognized me from the episode when I shot Carolyn Wolfe in the throat and remembered where I lived.

My mother was mad at me, all right, but she seemed

even madder at the cops for parking their squad car in front of our house where the neighbors could see it and gossip about what was going on at the Murphy house this time. She told me she was going to teach me a lesson about not running away from home, but I really didn't know what she meant. I wasn't running away. I was just going to visit my brother, something I thought she should have done.

As usual, my mother yelled at me for having mortified her and, as usual, I had no clue what mortified meant – what kid my age did? But I could tell, from her tone of voice, it wasn't anything good. The only good part was that the cops didn't cuff me so I didn't look like a death row convict when I got out of their car; my mother would have gone totally bonkers if the cops brought me home wearing handcuffs. She was so mad at me that she was shaking and kept saying, 'I'll teach you what it's like to run away from home, just you wait and see!'

As it turned out, on the very next day she abandoned me, intentionally, among hundreds of shoppers inside the downtown Chicago department store known as Marshall Field's. Until that day I loved going to Marshall Field's because the toy department had a magical display of Lionel, electric trains with lights, water, grass, trees, roads, bridges, tunnels and buildings. It looked like a miniature town and was the most exciting toy display I'd ever seen. Once, when my father and I had been watching the train whiz around the tracks, the engine jumped the tracks on a curve and to my amazement, my father caught it before it hit the floor. The other shoppers who were watching gave my father a round of applause, which made me proud of him like I was when he successfully replaced the engine onto the track and reconnected it to the rest of the train. It was the first time I thought of him as a hero.

So, on the day after the cops brought me home from walking the railroad tracks, my mother and I got off an elevator at Marshall Field's toy department, and as I would painfully learn, it wasn't just to watch the electric trains. She intended to ditch me there to teach me how it felt to be lost. After I'd watched the train going around until I was dizzy, I realized my mother was gone. I raced around the toy department looking for her, but she was nowhere to be found. Suddenly, in addition to teaching me how being lost felt, I was learning how it felt to have a panic attack.

Of course, I didn't know anything about panic attacks then, I just knew it was the most frightening thing I'd ever experienced. I was shaking like a leaf and crying like a baby as I hunted all over the store for her. I had trouble catching my breath and when I took deep breaths, I'd get dizzy. I thought she didn't want me anymore and I was scared stiff wondering about who would take care of me.

An older man with dark brown skin, dressed in a dark blue, wrinkled uniform, who said he was a guard, took me by my right hand, led me onto an elevator and told the elevator operator to take us to the second floor. That only made things worse for me because my mother had told me that if I misbehaved at Marshall Field's, the boogieman would push me down an elevator shaft and I'd be crushed to death. So, getting on an elevator with some older man I didn't know only scared me worse. By the time my mother showed up at the lost and found office to claim me, I was doomed to take the terror of being abandoned to my grave. But at that time, she didn't seem to care much about my feelings.

As frightening as that experience was, at least it was over the same day it began. But there was another time when my parents ditched me with a couple I'd just met, Gert and Dave J. My father met Dave at the Park Ridge group of Alcoholics Anonymous, where the custom was to refer to one another by first names plus the first initials of last names.

My parents left me at the J's house, told me to behave, and said they'd be back soon to get me, but it never occurred to me that their idea of soon was sometime next month. To me, soon meant hours, not weeks! What kid in his right mind would have thought anything else under the circumstances? By nightfall, I became desperate to go home and there was nothing to do at the J's house except listen to the radio. There were no kids or pets to play with, not even a goldfish, and the house had a peculiar odor like the bottom of my mother's birdcage. Mrs. J said the smell was from boiling cabbage. She had buck teeth, awful breath, frizzy gray hair and bulging eyes, but she was really nice to me. She even made me a root beer float with Borden's vanilla ice cream and Dad's Old Fashioned root beer. I don't know why but she called it a 'black cow' and it was delicious.

I couldn't get a straight answer from her about when my parents were coming back to take me home and I was getting more scared by the minute. I still have a memory of sitting on the staircase to their second floor and shaking like I was inside a refrigerator because I didn't even know how to get to our house from their house.

Mrs. J finally caved into my tearful nightfall cross examination, admitted the truth, and I freaked out. Not only did she tell me I was going to be there for a couple of weeks, but she also said she had no way of contacting my parents because they were driving to Boston, and she didn't know where they would be or when. I'd never felt that alone and scared in my life.

By the time I found out from her about the mystery trip, my parents could have been somewhere in Ohio, eating at a roadside diner, one of those places with a deer head mounted on a wall made with knotty pine boards, or searching for a motel with a blinking, red neon vacancy sign. There was no way to call them. I'd have to wait for them to get to a phone booth so they could call me, and I was praying that they would so I wouldn't be so scared. My father finally called and told me if I stopped crying, he'd bring me a nice present when they came back, maybe an Indian headdress with lots of feathers.

To me, the whole thing translated to only one reasonable conclusion, that they'd gone to Boston so they could visit with Jimmy at the hospital in Holyoke, and they didn't want me to go, or that I'd been given up for adoption because of the trouble I'd caused. Walking the train tracks might have been the straw that broke the camel's back. What convinced me was the fact that I was the only one left with the Js, and not my sisters.

I was pretty sure that Dorothy and Barbara had gone with my parents to Boston, along with our brown and white dog and my mother's yellow canary. Without me, they probably had more room in the car for the birdcage. Or they really had given me up for adoption to the Js. Sometimes I felt like my mother liked the bird better than me.

Chapter Fifteen

Less Than True

I often sensed that nobody in the family liked me much, but I didn't think they disliked me enough to ditch me completely. If the family was on the way to Boston without me, it would have been totally unfair, especially if they were planning to reunite with Jimmy and leave me alone in Park Ridge. After all, I hated the Chicago area as much as the rest of them did. I wanted to go back to Boston just like they did. Heck, I'd been born in Boston, Dorchester actually, and had lived in Milton for three years before my father's company transferred us to Chicago, where I was never happy. Back to Boston without me? That was the meanest thing I'd ever heard! I was doubtful if a family reunion was ever going to happen and, by that time, I knew better than to get my hopes up about it.

Fortunately, in spite of my suspicions, my parents later made another phone call to the Js, spoke with me and promised that they were planning to come back. They never said a word about Jimmy, but I didn't know that I would have believed them anyway. I didn't quite get why yet, but much of what they told me was less than true, even when the truth was obvious.

Surprise, surprise – when my parents did return, Jimmy was with them! Not Dorothy and Barbara; I had no idea where they had been staying. But my parents promised me that the whole family would be back together, even the dog and the canary.

As upset as I'd been about being left behind without any warning, I was still glad to see my parents and absolutely thrilled to see Jimmy when the trip to Boston was over, even if nobody seemed as glad to see me. The two weeks my parents were away did nothing to strengthen my sense of trust in people. If you can't trust your parents, who can you trust?

Except for that, I don't remember Jimmy looking all that different except his teeth, although straight, looked like 'choppers,' my father's name for false teeth that looked like false teeth. But I think his speech was clearer, although still not normal. What troubled me was that his behavior wasn't as lively, and his sense of humor seemed to be missing. Jimmy wasn't as happy as when he left, and it wasn't as much fun being around him. I guess I was expecting a miracle to occur but… no miracle. I wondered what had been the use of sending him to Massachusetts for surgery and speech therapy. I thought he'd have been better off if he'd stayed in Chicago.

As for me, that wouldn't be the last time I'd feel unwanted, abandoned or untrusting, either, and the worst part was there was nothing I could do to change my parents, especially my mother. In her mind she was always right, and nothing ever seemed to change her opinion about herself. And there wouldn't be many times when my father would take my side, even when it would be obvious to everybody else that my mother was wrong. I couldn't even rely upon my siblings – my own brother and sisters – to stick up for me. It seemed like they were always waiting for a chance to harass me.

Take the time that my parents told me that they were going to visit some dentist named Dr. Norman, who lived on the south side of Chicago. My mother told me they'd be gone for several hours, and Dorothy, Jimmy and Barbara would take care of me. Well, I knew that the three of them were waiting to get even with me for something I'd done and if I was home with them, they'd make me miserable. So, I lied to my parents, telling them that a boy named Bobby Thompson who I knew from school had invited me to spend that Saturday at his house and I'd agreed.

I had been to his house once, so I knew where it was. When my parents asked for the address, I actually remembered it and I told my parents that his parents were going to give me a ride home. To my surprise, my father said he'd drop me off there and my mother could talk to Bobby's mother to be sure everything was okay.

When we got to his house, I went to the front door and rang the doorbell but there was no answer, and the door was locked. So, I told my mother that his mother was taking a shower and assured her that I was welcome to stay, and the Thompsons would bring me home. To my amazement, my parents believed me and left me there. That might have been the last time they believed anything I told them!

After a while it started to rain and there was no place that I could keep dry. But I noticed that the window in Bobby's bedroom was open, so I climbed up the tree outside of it. Unfortunately, I was wearing my leather school shoes and lost my footing on the wet bark. During the fall, my face hit the bottom tree branch and blood spurt out of my nose like it was our garden hose. I couldn't make the bleeding stop and even though it was still raining, I began walking home.

Several times, cars on West Touhy Avenue stopped to ask me if I needed help but I kept walking. My parents had drilled into my head that I was never to get into someone's car if I didn't know who they were. As I entered the front door to our house, Barbara saw me and saw the blood. She screamed to Dorothy that I'd been hit by a car and Dorothy came running downstairs carrying a box of small size Band-Aids as if they would stop the bleeding. The two of them helped get me cleaned up and helped me put on dry clothes.

But when my parents got home, they could see I'd had an accident, and I had to admit that I'd lied to them. My mother shouted in my ear the usual threats about going to jail, going to hell and whatever other nutty things she usually came up with. But she hadn't yet threatened me with the really scary stuff. That wouldn't happen for another year or two. That would be when her threats would become frighteningly brutal, and I'd become terrified of the things she might do to punish me.

There were so many screwy events that happened during the years we lived in Park Ridge, that it's a wonder any of us were sane. Like the time that my father won a live, twenty-pound turkey in a raffle at an AA meeting. He brought the thing home in his car and put it in our garage. That made my mother furious, and she started yelling that she didn't need anything else to feed and clean up after. The hollering woke me up and I ran downstairs in time to hear her make some snotty remark about the turkey's 'drinking problem.'

To tell you the truth, I didn't know what she was talking about but when my father asked her what in hell she was raving about this time, she replied, 'Why else would a turkey be at an AA meeting?' That made my father so hot under the collar that his face turned red and the blood vessels in his temples began throbbing. It looked like a Jim Murphy explosion was coming and it did. He told her she was the dizziest dame he'd ever met. Her reply was, 'I may be dizzy, but you're stupid. You told me that new AA members are called pigeons and now you bring a turkey home. You don't even know the difference between a pigeon and a turkey!'

I didn't know if she was kidding or delirious. All I knew was that she was mad. I thought there was going to be a fist fight any minute and I ran upstairs to my bedroom, closed the bedroom door and prayed that my father wouldn't wind up sleeping in my bed again, like he sometimes did before he stopped drinking.

The next day I named the gobbler Birdie and began treating it like a family pet. I brought it some canary seed, bread scraps and a bowl of water. The following day, when I checked the garage to be sure there was enough food and water, Birdie was gone. A few hours later, my father returned with what was left of Birdie. It looked like it could have been the head from Ichabod Crane's horseman, and it was almost as smooth as an egg. The bald bird's body looked more like an overinflated football, about ready to burst, than a turkey. What had been my new pet emerged from our oven the next morning, after being cooked for seven hours at 325 degrees, as the featured menu item for our Thanksgiving dinner. That was the only meatless Thanksgiving dinner I'd ever eaten. I was so upset about my father having the bird decapitated that it's a miracle I didn't become a vegetarian for the rest of my life.

I'll have to say this, though, dealing with my mother's peculiarities, anger and punishment didn't quite prepare me for dealing with the nuns at parochial school. What a shock it was when I came up against a militant army of nuns, brandishing wooden rulers with sharp metal edges. Going to parochial school reminded me of a newsreel I'd seen about a World War II prisoner of war camp. The experience was pretty frightening from the first moment I stepped into the school. If you never experienced parochial school back in the day, the only thing comparable that comes to mind is basic training for military duty.

Chapter Sixteen

Parochial Perils

If I thought walking the rails toward Boston had upset my mother, that was nothing compared to the near-death incident that happened when I was almost six and entered the 1st grade at St. Paul of the Cross School in Park Ridge, the start of my parochial perils. My mother had this crazy idea that putting me in a parochial school would keep me out of trouble. Her oldest sister, my aunt Katie, the nun whom I'd never met, had convinced her to enroll me in a parochial school but it wasn't long before my mother regretted that decision. It happened when a kid in the 4th grade, whom I'd never heard of, climbed a telephone pole next to the school yard to prove that he was braver than the rest of us. Supposedly, he was pretending to be 'Tarzan, the jungle boy,' and said he could climb poles and trees better than anybody else.

While that probably was true, he should have brought a parachute with him because, when he reached the top of the pole, he tried to impersonate Tarzan by standing upright and flexing his biceps. One of my classmates said the kid lost his footing and fell headfirst to his death. I wasn't there to see it, but I heard about it through the grapevine from the other kids. We'd always hear about important things that way at school. My mother insisted that I'd been too close for comfort to the place where he died. What the heck did that mean? I wasn't even there when it happened.

The reason I wasn't there was that I'd played hooky that day by hiding in the bushes at the school bus stop, across the street from our house. I didn't think my mother would know the difference. Little did I know, she always watched me from our living room window until she saw me get on the bus. For some forgotten reason, that day there was only a half day of classes, so I'd figured I wouldn't miss much. When the school bus later returned and dropped the other kids off, I casually walked into our kitchen like nothing was wrong.

That was when I found out the school had called my mother to report that I never showed up. When my mother asked me how school was, I said, 'Great.' She went ballistic about my lie. I tried to talk my way out of it by saying someone at school must have made a mistake. Only a moron would have told her another lie. That was when she went double nuts and told me she had seen me hiding in the bushes instead of getting on the bus. At that point my goose was cooked and she sent me to bed for the rest of the day. I probably didn't even get fed, knowing her. She later said, 'You're not smart enough to pull the wool over my eyes.' It wasn't until I got to school the next day that I heard the story about the telephone pole catastrophe and the death of Tarzan, the jungle boy.

Someone started a rumor that the kid's death wasn't accidental; he'd committed suicide because the nuns had been whacking him in the head with rulers for four years. They whacked a lot of the kids, at least a lot of the boys. Anyway, the 4th grader's death incident convinced my mother that she couldn't trust the nuns to protect me. I could have told her that after the first week of school and my first wrestling match with Sister Mary Dominic. My mother already knew that she couldn't trust me, so she made it clear, following the kid's funeral, that she'd be watching me, she said, 'like a hawk.' I wasn't sure if that meant like she was the hawk or I was, but it didn't sound like anything good. But still my mother left me there, in spite of the danger.

My 1st grade teacher, Sister Mary Dominic, was larger than most of the nuns and was an imposing figure in her black uniform. Decades later, when I would see the Star Wars movie character, Darth Vader, it would remind me of my first impression of Sister Mary Dominic. But she had a pleasant face and wore rimless eyeglasses that softened her appearance. I had a feeling that under all that nun garb she might have been a nice person. But she looked something like an evil comic book character because of her black hood, cape and habit. I thought she was younger than most of the nuns, but it was hard to tell. Surprisingly, unlike most of the nuns, she even smiled once in a while.

Her ruler had a clearly intimidating and prominent place of distinction on her desk. I always knew when she was thinking about whacking somebody because she'd take the ruler in one hand and start slapping it against the palm of her other hand as a warning. If that didn't get the desired result, she'd smack it against the top of her desk, which made a really loud noise and it got worse when it echoed off the blackboard. Sometimes that left my ears ringing.

If all else failed, she'd go into battle mode, walk over to the troublemaker's desk and smack the kid on the hand or arm or wherever she could find bare skin to make sure he got her message. Or she'd call him up to her desk and deliver the punishment right there in front of the whole class. I think it was always one of the boys that caused trouble. I can't remember a girl ever getting whacked with the ruler. Actually, I can't remember it happening all that often, but I worried about it all the time.

What I remember most is the first time Sister Mary Dominic came to my desk. She hovered over me, then bent down to scold me for making marks in a pamphlet she had passed out. I thought she had given it to me and didn't know I couldn't draw on it. Her long black veil that covered her head fell forward like a drape and surrounded me in semi-darkness, like there was an eclipse of the sun. The whole thing was pretty spooky. When that happened, I ducked down and tried to get away from her, but she grabbed me in a head lock and suddenly it seemed that I was in a wrestling match.

The constant threat of punishment at home was bad enough, but combined with the threat at school, I was nervous about being reprimanded all the time. My sister Barbara used to say that I was my mother's pet, which was ridiculous because, if I was, I must have been a pet skunk. At parochial school, nobody confused me with being the teacher's pet. Before long I became one of the school's criminal element and Sister Mary Dominic's enemy.

The kid's wake was ghastly. Everyone in the school had to parade past his body, lying in a shiny mahogany casket where a brown wooden crucifix with a silver Jesus was attached to the white pleated cloth inside the open cover. The casket looked like the trunk of our car whenever my father opened it, except it was much cleaner and didn't have a spare tire, a jack, a tire iron and battery jumper cables. The dead kid was wearing a white shirt and a black necktie. I couldn't tell if he had any pants on or underwear for that matter because his legs were under a blanket.

The dead kid's hands were folded, one over the other and were holding a string of rosary beads. I can't for the life of me remember his name, which is odd because people say I have a good memory. It was practically impossible to believe that he was dead, except that the skin on his hands looked kind of rubbery, like the gloves that my mother used when she washed dishes. His face looked like it had some of my mother's makeup powder on it, mostly where his forehead must have hit the asphalt pavement. When I paused at the kneeler to pray, I thought about poking him in the shoulder to see if he'd wake up. But I knew the nuns would have a conniption if I did. In parochial school you had to be careful about doing anything that hadn't been approved by the nuns or, as some kids called them, the penguin colony, because of their black and white outfits.

We were ordered to take a good look at the dead kid, then pray the Our Father and the Hail Mary. At the funeral Mass, Father Smith, the pastor, gave us a speech about not climbing telephone poles, not touching electrical wires and some other dangers about disobeying school rules. Then the principal, aka Mother Superior, who was nastier than the rest of the nuns, talked about a bunch of new rules at the school. Oh, brother, the last thing that place needed was more rules so, as usual, I tuned her out and started daydreaming about electric trains and toy soldiers.

Truthfully, though, I was scared to death of the principal. Some of the kids in my class called her Sister Adolph Hitler, but she reminded me more of the wicked witch in some scary Disney movie. She dressed like the other nuns at the school, with a black headdress shaped like a shoebox standing upright, a drape attached to the top of it and a starched white contraption with an opening that surrounded her face. The white contraption was attached to a starched white bib under her chin; it was at least two feet long. If you looked at her a certain way, it looked like she got her head stuck in a toilet seat.

She wore a black full-length dress called a habit and black ankle-high shoes with laces. When she turned her head, that starched face contraption sometimes made the skin on her cheeks puff out like she was a squirrel with a mouthful of acorns. She was thin and her face was wrinkled up like a prune. My mother made me eat prunes all the time, so I knew what a prune looked like,

and it wasn't pretty. To me, those nun get-ups looked ridiculous, like they were military uniforms from the Dark Ages.

When the principal marched down the corridors, you could hear her coming a mile away because her shoes had leather heels that banged against the wooden floors like somebody was hammering nails. Then there were the gigantic rosary beads she wore around her waist that clattered like the tail of a rattlesnake warning everyone that danger was near and, believe me, in her case it was.

I still remember her frisking some of us kids to be sure we weren't stealing school supplies. There was nothing that made me cringe as much as her wiggling her boney fingers around inside the pockets of my corduroy pants. Then she'd pat down my pant legs like she was a cop, and I was a robber. I was afraid she might make me strip to my underwear in front of everyone in the class and once she threatened to do just that.

The Catholic Church should have made it a mortal sin for nuns to frisk students. That was seriously embarrassing, especially for boys, and I have to admit that I turned into a cringing coward whenever Sister Adolph showed up. Between Sister Mary Dominic and the principal, St. Paul of the Cross was like being in a prisoner-of-war camp.

As things turned out, my mother should have hired a private eye to follow me around after the funeral. I got suspended from parochial school before the end of 1st grade for swiping puzzle pieces from Sister Mary

Dominic's classroom, not because I wanted the puzzles but because I disliked her and Sister Adolph. My mother was furious because the suspension prevented me from going to school on the day of the class picture. You'd have thought I committed a bank robbery, judging by her reaction. What was really weird was that she would keep that class picture in her hope chest until Dorothy would eventually steal it, even though I wasn't in it, and neither she nor my mother knew anybody who was except Sister Mary Dominic.

Chapter Seventeen

Suicide doors

Of all the events that happened when I was in 1st grade, none compared with the winter day when we'd had about two feet of snow overnight. School had been cancelled and my parents decided to do some shopping once the roads had been ploughed. That was before snow tires were popular if even available – tire chains were the best choice. Even though my father kept a set of chains in the trunk of his car, he was too impatient to install them. So, off we went in his gray Dodge sedan, headed toward Chicago, slipping and sliding from one side of the road to the other.

The roads were icy all right, but my father ignored my mother's warnings about getting into an accident. That was no surprise to me. Even though she'd never driven, she was an expert at criticizing other people's driving. She used to routinely say to him, 'You should be a racecar driver at the Indianapolis Speedway. If you want to kill yourself, fine! But don't kill the rest of us because you're nuts!'

His response was, 'They call people like you backseat drivers so why the hell are you sitting up front? How about getting in the back and opening one of the doors the next time you think I'm going too fast? Maybe that will shut you up.' Although I'd once heard him call the back doors suicide doors, I wasn't sure what he meant. Most times I tuned them out when they were arguing but I was curious about what he meant about opening a back door while the car was moving. I didn't know that was possible.

But I soon would learn that it meant the rear doors opened in the opposite direction than the car was traveling. I vaguely remembered someone mentioning it but I couldn't resist opening one of them just to see what all the fuss was about. What normal kid wouldn't?

We were zooming down Northwest Highway at about fifty miles per hour when I lifted the latch button on the door next to me and quietly eased the door handle ever so slowly upward. Once the wind caught the edge of the door, the rest was like a war scene from a movie. There was an explosion that went 'KA-BOOM' and felt like a German U-boat torpedo had struck the Dodge broadside. It definitely was the loudest noise I'd ever heard, and the explosion momentarily lifted the front end of the car off the road. The wind nearly yanked the door off its hinges, me along with it. For a few seconds I was still attached to the door, squeezing the handle for dear life while shouting, 'WHOA!'

The next thing I knew, the car swerved left, and I swerved right, flying off into space like the guy that gets shot out of a cannon at the circus. I might have been killed except for the four-feet high pile of freshly ploughed snow that knocked the wind out of me when I landed. My brother thought that was the funniest thing ever, funnier than the time I fell out of the tree at Bobby Thompson's house, smashed my nose on the bottom branch and looked like the lone survivor of an airplane crash landing.

Those kinds of behaviors used to freak my mother out and she developed a much more militant attitude about me. I guess I shouldn't blame her. Sometimes I did really dopey things. In her world, each one of my antics was another crisis in her growing list of misdemeanors and felonies in the crime spree of her juvenile delinquent son, Bobby, the child she feared would grow-up to be a mobster like Al Capone – that is, if I ever survived childhood.

Although my father was more inclined to forgive and forget, my mother became more tightly wrapped. She repeatedly told me that I'd never get to be a doctor if I had a criminal record. That was strange because I don't know what made her think I wanted to be a doctor. She also told me I'd be doomed to jail or hell if I kept misbehaving. She claimed that the family would be cursed with misfortune, illness and death because of my sinfulness. Either my father's drinking problem would return because of the trouble I caused, or someone would be cursed with some deadly disease like cancer because of me, or someone would get killed in an accident that would be my fault.

I'd be lying if I denied that her threats bothered me. Actually, they scared the crap out of me sometimes and even though I hardly knew yet what anxiety was, I had it! My mother kept telling me that I was evil, but I didn't know what to do about it except pray a lot. That's what I did, I prayed a lot.

Meanwhile, my mother was terrified that sooner or later the neighbors might learn the whole truth about my absurd behavior and circulate a petition demanding that we move out of the neighborhood, maybe to a different state or to a foreign country. If my mother's suspicions were correct, the neighbors' wishes were about to come true.

Then came the Friday afternoon when I was catty corner from our house, at the house owned by the Ramseys on the other side of the crossroads of South Greenwood Avenue and South Arthur. Their red brick garage contained all the Illinois license plates that they'd ever owned, and I used to go there to study them. I liked to run my fingers over the numbers with my eyes closed to see if I could guess them all. I heard Barbara calling my name and when I walked outside, here she comes, all excited about something. 'Get home and pack your stuff,' she said, almost out of breath. 'We're moving back to Boston!'

WOWSER-DOWSER! That was the best news ever, but I was concerned if I was going or being left behind. Barbara said everyone except Dorothy was going. Dorothy was not invited because she had a fierce argument with our mother about something and she was told to move out of the house and to never come back.

It was only a few days before the Allied Van Lines moving truck pulled up to our house and three workers started emptying everything out of the house and into the truck. The truck was painted orange with black, yellow and white lettering on the sides. The three moving men filled the truck in a day and before dark, the truck headed off to Boston. The rest of us, dog and canary included, but without Dorothy, headed out the following morning after sleeping in a motel on the Indiana side of Chicago.

Chapter Eighteen

A can of sardines

The return trip to the Boston area seemed to take forever even though it was only three days. Even without Dorothy, the rest of us were squeezed into the Dodge like it was a can of sardines, probably because Barbara and I were bigger than we had been four years earlier when we moved to Chicago. My father insisted on stopping in Rochester, New York to visit the home office of his employer, The Ritter Company. While he spent hours inside the factory, the rest of us sat in the car, baking in the August sunshine of a parking lot. I remember my mother getting so mad that she went into the factory to find my father and when they both returned, they argued for hours about her embarrassing him in front of his bosses. As we headed for Boston, we got more excited by the mile. But I couldn't get Dorothy off my mind.

I knew what it felt like to be abandoned but Dorothy was more abandoned than I had been; more like what happened to Jimmy. She had no other family in Park Ridge other than us, not even a distant relative. And where would she live? Some things my parents did made me fearful; others made me angry. Dorothy's situation made me feel some of both. I couldn't do anything about it either. I had no control over that situation and hardly any other one.

The Beechwood Knoll was the name of the neighborhood where our new house was located. My father drove past Wollaston Beach on the way there. I couldn't believe we were going to live within sight and walking distance of a beach and near enough to the city of Boston to see the skyline across the bay. My father said Wollaston Beach was 'just a hop skip and a jump away' from Boston and was part of the city of Quincy. He said Wollaston was a postal zone of Quincy, something I'd never heard of before. At least he didn't mention a 'Wanted Dead or Alive' poster of me being at the post office in Wollaston, like he had said about the poster he claimed was at the post office in Park Ridge. By the end of the day, I'd met some of the neighborhood kids and learned that Quincy was a famous city and had lots of places to see and things to do, none of which I had ever seen or done when we lived in Park Ridge.

Things like the Atlantic Ocean, the Blue Hills, the Fore River Bridge, the Neponset River Bridge, a granite quarry, two yacht clubs at Wollaston Beach and a chain of barrier islands separating Quincy Bay from the Atlantic Ocean. And the yacht clubs were surrounded by motorboats and sail boats waiting to be enjoyed by their owners. There were two drive-in movie theatres nearby, a roller-skating rink and bowling alleys, There were kids talking to the movers who were waiting for us to arrive. Those kids told me there was a place called Squantum Naval Air Station nearby where airplanes took off and landed all day long. They told me about two metal drawbridges, historic houses and monuments. Quincy sounded like a paradise compared to Park Ridge which was only known for having a drive-in movie theatre.

The new kids were named Donny Degan, Bobby Degan, Scuffy Williams, Baldy Williams and Mike Dolan. Mike lived in the next house on our side of Havilend Street, #22. The Williams kids lived at #36, two houses further up on the same side and the Degans lived across the street from them at #41. They described the bus stop diagonally across form our house, the local fishing hole named Sailors' Home Pond on Rice Road, Black's Creek that went under the Merrymount Bridge and where kids could take sailing lessons, Pine Island that could be reached by a rickety, wooden bridge and where there was space to camp-out and, most important of all, the sandlot baseball field up the dirt road at the end of Andrews Road, just across from the Sailors' Home Cemetery. To me, it sounded like a heaven for kids, especially for boys.

Our new house had a deck porch above the garage and there was a post card view of the bay from up there. Before we had moved in, we were visited by the Quincy Police who'd had a phone call from the Park Ridge Police. Obviously, I thought it had something to do with me, but it was about Dorothy for a change. I overheard one of the cops saying she had been hospitalized in Park Ridge and a doctor named Ethan Allen Brown needed my parents to call him to authorize treatment. I recognized the doctor's name because he had treated Dorothy for asthma in the past.

When the cops left, my father began yelling at my mother because she had refused to leave a forwarding address for Dorothy. Dorothy had become ill and went to the house we'd lived in, but the new owners had no information. Dorothy had an asthma attack and was brought to the hospital by an ambulance. My father cussed-out my mother and left to make the phone call to Dr. Brown since we didn't have a phone yet. My parents were arguing already, and we hadn't even moved in. One of the kids who was watching asked me if my parents fought like that all the time. He said they must have been Irish, and I told him they were.

When my father returned, he told my mother that he'd agreed to pay for Dorothy's medical treatment and to buy her a bus ticket to get her from Park Ridge to Quincy. It was another incident that made me realize that confronting my mother, even for Dorothy, was a mistake. But I was still a slow learner because I never mastered the technique of getting along with her.

Actually, there were more stories about the things to do in the neighborhood like sitting on the stone wall at the beach during the sailboat races, watching the Navy planes taking-off and landing at the air station, being part of the Massachusetts Fields School Pet Stock Show every spring and the Fourth of July Parade that was the biggest deal ever.

The night of the Fourth, there'd be a neighborhood block party on Havilend Street where there was food and drinks along with music and dancing in the street. Who ever heard of things like that? Not me! The kids also raved about the fireworks display that took place at Merrymount Beach and lasted about a half-hour. It all sounded too good to be true, not to mention that there was also a Howard Johnson's ice cream stand at the beach during the summer. The original location was at the Wollaston train station. Howard Johnson, himself, lived up on Wollaston Hill.

My mother was thrilled to learn that there were delivery men who came to the knoll on a regular basis. There were milk deliveries, bread deliveries, a fruit and vegetable truck, a van from a dry-cleaning company, a diaper service and even a rag man with a horse and wagon. When we lived in Park Ridge there was nothing that compared for home deliveries.

What there wasn't was school bus service which we had in Park Ridge. So, in Wollaston we had to walk to school and home daily. I walked with the other kids from the neighborhood. We must have looked something like an ant farm on schooldays as we headed to and from our elementary school on Beach Street. It didn't matter what the weather was, we walked to school, in heat or cold, sleet or snow, rain or shine.

Just before reaching the brown brick, school building, we had to pass Mac's Variety store which was on the opposite side of Beach Street from the front of the school. Mac and his wife were both about five feet tall and could barely be seen over the glass candy counter. Mac's had a great collection of penny candy and gum. My favorites were Mint Juleps, Banana Splits and Double Bubble. My mother gave me a nickel to buy a container of milk at lunch but some days I'd use the nickel for candy and hope that she didn't find out.

Chapter Nineteen

Stick 'em up

After moving 1100 miles east to Quincy, who knew I'd get suspended from public school during 2nd grade? This time it was for bringing my father's thirty-two caliber pistol to school and scaring some snobby 6th grade girl that my new friends didn't like. It's hard for me to believe that I really pointed my father's pistol at someone and said, 'Stick 'em up,' but I really did!

The fact that I'd been thrown out of two schools in two states in two years seemed to push my mother off the deep end. Even though I didn't miss the class picture during the second suspension, my mother went nuts because she was forced to return early from a February vacation trip to Chicago. When she got home, she found out that my antics had become a hot news item around town, including the Quincy Patriot Ledger newspaper. I guess you could say that I'd become famous, or maybe notorious. According to the school grapevine, I was a celebrity.

I liked Mass. Fields School; it felt friendlier than St. Paul of the Cross. Maybe the best part was the absence of any nuns. Mrs. Ripley, my 2nd grade teacher, was a short, roly-poly, pleasant woman and my friend until the day when we were told to bring into school Show and Tell items about the Navajo Indians. I wanted to make a good impression and I knew where my father kept his pistol, the gun with the Indian on both sides of the handle. The words, Savage Arms, were pressed into both sides of the handle surrounding a side view of an Indian head with a feather headdress.

When my parents weren't home, I used to get the pistol out of its hiding place, stand in front of a mirror pointing the gun and pretending I was sticking up someone. Naturally, after all that practice, I thought that bringing the pistol to school was one of the most brilliant ideas I'd ever had. When I left the house, I tucked the pistol under my coat so nobody else would see it, including the house sitter, Mrs. James, who was staying at our house while my parents were on vacation. What could have been more perfect for teaching school kids about Indians than a pistol with an

Indian head?

Unfortunately for me, I told the other kids that I had a gun and my friends pulled and tugged on my coat until it came open and the pistol was in plain view. It looked awesome and one of the kids begged me to 'pull a stick-up.' Someone said, 'How about sticking up that tall, snobby, 6th grade bully, Sandra what's-her-name, who thinks she's better than the rest of us.' Most of the other guys agreed and some of them spread out around the school yard looking for Sandra.

When Mikey McNeice found her, he convinced her to see what I'd brought to school. When she came closer, I walked up to her, took out the pistol, pointed it up at her nose, which was about a foot higher than mine, and said, 'Stick 'em up, honey, and give me all your money.' I thought that was pretty clever because it rhymed. But I knew it was a mistake as soon as Sandra let out the wildest scream I'd ever heard and started running away in every direction at once.

She disappeared into a house on Rawson Road, and I figured, with my luck, that someone was going to call the Quincy Police... and someone did! I guess I could have told Sandra that the gun wasn't loaded and avoided a lot of trouble but that would have ruined all the fun. First thing I did when I got to class was to put the pistol on Mrs. Ripley's desk and say, 'Show and Tell.' You should have seen the look of terror that came over my teacher's face!

It seemed like only a minute or two before two Quincy cops walked into the classroom. Each one of them had his right hand on the pistol holstered on his

gun belt. One of the girls in the room screamed. Mrs. Ripley spoke up and told everyone to be calm. She picked-up the pistol by sticking her yellow number two pencil through the trigger guard and held it out to the cops. One of them took it, asked her something, and she pointed at me. Of course, who else would it have been, other than me? Next thing I knew, I was being taken into custody and marched out of class.

That was so embarrassing that I almost croaked. It seemed that everything I did led to more trouble. On that particular occasion I was taken to the office of Mr. Morrison, the school principal. After I confessed that my parents were in Chicago and Mrs. James, the visiting nanny couldn't drive, the cops agreed to drive me home. They took my father's pistol with them when we left the school for my house. I worried about Mrs. James, thinking she might pass out when the cops told her about the stick-up. Here I was again with cops. I thought our neighbors would be sure to think that I was a troublemaker.

Mr. Morrison was a short, thin, bald, bespectacled man who liked to wear bow ties, suits and vests. He'd said that I was suspended from school until my parents came home. One of them would have to bring me to the school for a meeting with the police and him. Holy crap, what a colossal mess this had turned out to be. When Mrs. James called my parents to tell them the news, she said that she wanted to leave when my mother told her there were two more pistols in the house and I knew where they were. When Barbara came home from school, she got Mrs. James to agree to stay with me until my parents came home. As a result, my mother had to catch the next train to Boston.

Not only was she enraged when the taxicab left her off at our front door, but she refused to speak to me at all. I was used to her screaming in my ear, but the silent treatment was a new tactic. Believe me, I knew that she was planning to get even with me some way, but I had no clue about how, when or where. Although nothing happened immediately, when it did, not only was it downright nasty but it was way worse than anything I'd imagined.

My father arrived a day or two later. When he took me to the meeting with Mr. Morrison, there was a Quincy Police motorcycle parked outside and a police officer named Earl Huntoon was introduced to us by Mr. Morrison. Officer Huntoon was a big man with blond hair. There weren't many times that my father had to look up at other people, but this was one. Officer Huntoon read my father the riot act, which included criticizing him for failing to register the pistol at the police station. He ordered my father to go to the police station after our meeting. Before my father left the school, he told me he'd have much more to say to me later... no doubt something about what a dope I was, not that I hadn't heard it all before. It was embarrassing but nothing compared to what was going to happen after the school year ended.

Chapter Twenty

Gates Of Hell

It was the Saturday morning after 2nd grade let out for the year and my parents ordered me to get into the backseat of my father's Buick because there was a place that they wanted me to see. That's all they would say about it, and I wasn't expecting anything good. The ride took about a half-hour, and I kept asking, over and over, where we were going because I was getting a very bad feeling about it. My father finally said, 'If you don't shut up, it will be the gates of hell.' I didn't believe his answer but, as it turned out, where we went was practically the same thing.

We drove up Quincy Shore Drive and over the Neponset River Bridge into Dorchester until we reached our destination – the Mattapan Mental Hospital where we drove through a pair of black steel gates at a guard house. My father told the guard that we were there to visit a patient and we were allowed to drive into the courtyard. I had no idea who it was that we came to see and when I asked my mother, she said it wasn't for them to see anyone – it was for me to see what the rest of my life would be like if they had to leave me there.

To say I was being terrorized was an understatement. My father took us for a tour of the red brick buildings and the grounds while my mother pointed out some of the 'loonies' as she called them. I figured that must have been where Nutsy Fagan, the crazy guy from my mother's childhood neighborhood wound up. She often called me Nutsy Fagan when she threatened to send me there.

Along came a group of five patients wearing pajamas and bath robes. They were shuffling along, being watched by two guys in white uniforms who my mother called orderlies. I wondered how she knew so much about the place. I'd never heard about any of that stuff. My father stopped the car to give us a better look at the mental patients, shuffling along, staring at the ground and mumbling – one looked like he was drooling.

I started crying on the inside, but I knew better than to let my father see me crying. My mother was telling me that the shufflers were people who had disobeyed their mothers and 'getting locked up' was what would happen to me if I kept doing things like pointing guns at people. She said if they left me there, I'd never see them or my brother and sisters again... never! That was the coldest, darkest moment I'd had yet, but there were worse things to come.

My father told me that he'd take me home only if I promised not to do any more 'numbskull' stunts. Of course, I promised but I didn't know there were more conditions to the deal. I should have known; there always were more conditions with my parents.

One condition was that I had to go with my mother to a doctor to inquire about some operation her sister, Katie, the nun, had suggested to calm me down. It was a good thing that I didn't know what they were planning to do to me, or I probably would have run away. My mother told me that she was going to have me fixed because I'd never get to be a doctor if I had a criminal record. I don't know what made her think I wanted to be a doctor in the first place. In the second place, I was only seven and probably wouldn't have understood what the heck she was talking about anyway.

The doctor's office was across from St. Ann's Rectory on Hancock Street, in Wollaston, where a man named Dr. Dalton was going to do what had been recommended by Katie, the nun, to make me more obedient and keep me out of trouble. But I didn't trust Dr. Dalton from the git-go. For one thing, his office was so dark it was spooky. For another, he was pretty decrepit looking, and I thought he was too old to be a doctor. He was tall, thin, wrinkled, hunched over and his hands were kind of shaky. He had a full head of gray hair, a bushy moustache and eyeglasses but he just seemed pretty old to be a doctor. Plus, his office was in the living room of an apartment and when I had to take my pants off so he could examine my groin, he had to shine a flashlight on me to see enough to decide about something or other and the shades in his front windows were open so anyone walking by could have seen me naked. The outcome of that visit was going to convince me that I never wanted anything more to do with doctors... never!

After my mother made a plan with him, she and my father drove me to Dorchester on a dreary Sunday evening a few weeks later. After we'd passed row after row of three-decker houses, we arrived at the Carney Hospital, where my father promised me 'faithfully' that nothing bad was going to happen to me while I was there, even though I was going to stay there overnight. What a pile of crap that turned out to be. I already knew that my mother was an untruthful person but until now, I hadn't known my father to tell me many lies. That sure changed.

By the next day, I was doomed to be scared to death of doctors and hospitals for the rest of my life because my parents had signed me up for surgery! It wasn't until I was on an operating table, under a huge, bright, circular light and a nun shoved an ether mask over my face, that I realized something terrible was about to happen and did it ever. With what I knew about nuns, if I'd had any common sense, I'd have jumped off the table to run for my life. If only I'd known what was up, I'd probably have brought my father's pistol to the hospital for protection.

Imagine my horror when I woke up in a dim recovery room with the only light coming through a round window in the door that looked like a porthole in a ship. I was in excruciating pain and, when I looked down, I saw that there was a bulging bloody tourniquet where my legs met. Even though I was in a fog, it only took a second to realize that the blood was mine.

I was totally freaked out because I had a habit of thinking the worst and the worst was that my mother had told the doctor to chop off something that I wanted to keep. She used to warn me regularly that she would have something like that done to me if I gave her

anymore trouble. Looking back, I couldn't believe that I hadn't made a getaway when I'd had the chance. Any kid with half a brain and an ounce of common sense would have known enough to run for his life.

When a nurse came into the recovery room, I could barely ask her what had happened to me because my mouth felt like it was full of cotton candy. I thought she said something about 'circle scissors,' which didn't make any sense when I first heard it, but after I put two and two together, I became hysterical. I was terrified that I was like Humpty Dumpty, and I couldn't be put together again. My biggest fear was that I'd never be able to have children.

Apparently, someone gave me knockout drops after that because I don't remember anything else until I woke up in my own bedroom a day later, wondering if it had all been a nightmare. A closer look at the bloody bandage together with the throbbing and excruciating pain confirmed that it hadn't been any dream.

Next morning, my mother gave me a sponge bath, dressed me in a short sleeve, white shirt and a pair of tan, short pants before combing my hair her way, except she left my cow lick sticking up. Then a photographer came to our front door to take a picture of me sitting on a striped red and white foot stool. I was still in pain, but I was the only one who cared about that. Days later when the photograph was delivered, my mother put it into an eight by ten-inch brass frame, after which it would be displayed in our living room forever, a constant reminder of her victory over a seven-year-old child.

And things weren't going to get better anytime soon, especially when my mother took me back to Dr. Dalton's office to have him yank out the stitches. That was some of the worst pain ever. I was terrified to watch what he was doing, especially since he was shaking more than I was. And all this because of a recommendation by Katie, the nun, whom I'd never met. If the surgery was supposed to calm me down, it was a total failure. I don't think I was ever calm after that catastrophe.

Fortunately, when the bandage was removed, I realized that I'd only lost some skin but, after that, whenever I'd go to a doctor's office or to a hospital, I'd be as nervous as a guy wearing a hangman's noose, waiting for the gallows platform to drop open and the noose to snap his neck like a turkey's wishbone on Thanksgiving.

What kind of parents would do that to a kid without preparing him for the ordeal and checking to see if it was okay with him? What kind of parents would promise a kid that nothing bad was going to happen when they knew perfectly well that he was going into surgery? I didn't know what to think. I felt like a prisoner of war. I knew I was going to have to work at avoiding my parents if I wanted to keep the rest of my body in one piece. Believe me, after going under the knife, I had more reason to fear my mother's behavior than she had to fear mine.

I couldn't believe my father was part of the plot. He was a guy and should have known that the surgery was going to be a shock to me when I saw the result. I'd never trust either of my parents again. My mother's favorite saying became, 'Someday, mister, we'll be visiting you in jail if they don't put you in the nuthouse first.' After that she continued calling me 'Nutsy Fagan,' that guy from her childhood neighborhood in Dorchester who turned out to really be nuts. That will give you some idea about her opinion of me.

According to my mother, if I didn't stop acting like a crazy person, trying to get my way and disobeying her, she would make sure that I spent the rest of my life at Mattapan. If my mother was trying to scare me straight, she was doing a darned good job because, after the surgery episode, I didn't doubt for a minute that she'd send me to another hospital, even Mattapan. That was never truer than the day she called telephone information to get the phone number for Mattapan.

I was stunned when my mother dialed the nuthouse and told someone there to send an ambulance, with a straitjacket, to take me away, lock me up and throw away the key. I'm not kidding, that's exactly what she said on the phone. I didn't think what I did was that big a deal, but my mother had a lot of rules and shooting a cap pistol inside the house was her pet peeve. I knew she'd go cuckoo if I shot it, so when I say it was an accident, believe me, it was an accident.

The cap pistol was a new gift from my father's oldest sister, Molly, an aunt I barely knew who lived in Montana. It was a full-size replica of a Colt, forty-five caliber, 6-shooter that had an imitation pearl handle, a revolving cartridge chamber and six imitation cartridges that fired circular caps. It was awesome, to say the least, and practically every kid in the neighborhood came to see it in action.

That all ended when I accidentally released the hammer and a cap exploded in our dining room. My mother ran down the stairs from her bedroom, grabbed the gun from me, opened the door to the basement and threw the pistol against the concrete basement wall with all her might. My precious pistol broke into pieces on the same day I got it and was way beyond repair. I hated to give my mother the satisfaction of seeing me cry, which I suspected was near the top of her list of favorite things. But destroying my new gun was way over the top of mean things to do and I began to cry my eyes out. I then had to listen to her telling me that the ruined gun was my fault and I had only myself to blame. I thought, why not? Everything else that went wrong seemed to be my fault.

During the phone call to Mattapan Hospital, she was so calm that you'd have thought she was ordering take-out chop suey from Star of the Sea Chinese restaurant. Me? I was about to drop dead from a heart attack or, at least, have a nervous breakdown while we waited for the ambulance with the straitjacket to arrive. I couldn't decide which was worse, smashing my pistol to pieces or calling the loony bin to come and take me away.

Meanwhile, my mother went through my drawers, picking out clean clothes for me to wear to the hospital. After I desperately pleaded for mercy over and over again, she finally called back to cancel the ambulance and my heart resumed beating. When it was over, I thought she'd never stop laughing. You might say that my mother's parenting style was pretty harsh and, based on what I'd seen, she was pretty good at it.

My mother also liked to scare me by coming up the stairs while I was falling asleep, pretending that she was the boogeyman. She had a bizarre routine of making her voice quiver while saying 'Bobby, I'm up one step, Bobby, I'm up two steps, Bobby, I'm up three steps,' and so on until she reached the top landing. By then, I would be partly awake, and she'd leap into my darkened bedroom, grab me by the throat and shout, 'Bobby, I've got you!' You-know-who thought that was hilarious, and it wasn't me.

Chapter Twenty-one

Revenge is sweet

Obviously, I didn't have much of a chance against my parents, my brother and my sisters. I seemed to clash with my mother and Barbara more often than the others. I realized that I gave my mother a lot of trouble, so I wasn't entirely surprised by the way she treated me. But Barbara? I just seemed to rub her the wrong way most of the time. I think there were two reasons for it. First, Barbara was often at home when I was there so we couldn't help bumping into each other. Second, she was forced to babysit for me, and she hated it.

When Barbara was babysitting for me, sometimes you'd have thought we were bitter enemies. Once I heard my father say that revenge is sweet. That idea was an answer to a prayer of mine, and I decided to hang on to that thought until just the right time when Barbara might say something that really disturbed me. I didn't have to wait for long.

Barbara loved to chit chat with her girlfriends on the yellow wall phone in our kitchen. She was sitting there on one of our kitchen chairs, facing away from the back door when I came home from the beach one day after Barbara embarrassed me in front of one of her high school friends. I'll always be grateful to Barbara for teaching me how to swim but she only did it because my mother insisted that she take me to the beach with her. Barbara thought if I learned to swim, I wouldn't be hanging around her as much.

Barbara usually called me 'the little pest' which was probably true. But then there was the time when she told her best friend, Jean, that I was a 'royal pain in the ass.' That was totally humiliating and reminded me of the time Jimmy called me a little asshole. What a terrible thing for her to say about me! So, I made up my mind that I would get even with Barbara somehow and, believe me, I did.

Between our back stairs and the bulkhead to the basement was a window well. Lo and behold, there were a dozen or so garter snakes in a ball, wriggling around inside the well when I came up the stairs. I had this stroke of genius to grab the biggest snake and scare Barbara because the two things she hated most in life

were mice and snakes. The biggest snake was no juvenile either. It was big enough to have been the mother of all garter snakes, with a thick body and a head large enough to swallow an adult frog in one gulp.

When I grabbed it, I opened the screen door as quietly as I could, tiptoed up behind my sister and dangled the black and yellow snake by its tail from above her head so that the snake's head dropped directly in front of her face. At first, she didn't realize what was happening until, that is, the snake looked her straight in the eye and flicked it's red and black tongue at her nose.

Barbara let out the scariest scream I'd ever heard, loud enough to scare everyone within a mile. Whatever singing voice was higher than soprano, she definitely hit it and maybe another one even higher! She turned pale as a ghost, jumped up, knocked the chair over, running out the back door like a wild person, frantically waving her arms around like she was a human helicopter and leaving the receiver of the yellow phone swinging in mid-air like a clock pendulum. That was the best prank I'd ever played on anyone, and I was laughing so hard that I accidentally dropped the snake on the kitchen floor, which terrified our dopey dog into running out the door after Barbara did, slipping and sliding like it was wearing ice skates. I was so happy that I said a prayer thanking God for helping me to get even.

I didn't know girls could scream that loud or high and I'd forgotten how fast Barbara could run. I didn't know that getting even could be so much fun. I still grin every time I think about it. Boy, did I get her good and she never forgot it. After that, I'd sometimes remind her to check under her bed for snakes at nighttime. Barbara seemed to have a healthier respect for me after that, but I knew better than to push my luck with her. How would I ever explain to my friends that my sister had beaten me up if she ever did? It had always been tough being the runt of the litter, but at least I was learning to stand up for myself. My parents grounded me for that one. I seemed to have a talent for getting into trouble doing just about everything, even ordinary stuff.

At the start of every summer, I'd head for the barber shop on Hancock Street with my friends. It was in the block of stores between Johnson's Filling Station and Metherall's Plumbing Supply. The Metheralls lived in our neighborhood across the street from the Degans' house. They had one of the few two-car garages. My mother ordered me to get a short haircut like the one Scuffy Williams had which was called a wiffle. Scuffy had a real name; it was Roger. He had brown hair and was forced to wear leg braces because he was recovering from infantile paralysis, better known as polio. He was called Scuffy because his shoes were scuffed from walking with braces.

His younger brother, Richard, had blond hair and when he got a wiffle, it looked like he didn't have any hair at all. So, he was called Baldy sometimes and that upset his mother. I remember the day she got in my face about it and told me to call him by his proper name. I wasn't mocking him – I just thought he liked being called Baldy. However, when Mrs. Dolan told my mother what had happened, my mother treated me like I was the one who gave him the nickname, although the other kids said it was Donny Degan. Nevertheless, my mother blamed me. She always seemed to enjoy blaming me for bad stuff.

Donny's younger brother was named Bobby. I think Bobby was a year older than me and Donny was two years older. The two of them seemed to get into fist fights with each other just about every day. Donny had red hair and my mother said that people with red hair tended to have short fuses which meant they were easily angered. My mother had a brother named Eddie whose hair was reddish blond, but he seemed pretty calm to me.

The last of the gang was Mike Dolan, who was blond and had longer hair than the rest of us. Mike was usually the butt of the Degans' jokes and ridicule, but he never seemed to mind it much. The thing I remember most about him was that he hated cutting his fingernails and they were usually gross looking. Mike and I didn't have much in common – I loved sports, he didn't. After my sister, Barbara, taught me how to swim, I went to the beach as often as I could. Mike didn't care much about swimming. I liked fishing mornings at Sailors' Home Pond, but Mike liked sleeping better. I liked traipsing through the marsh and netting minnows, Mike was careful about not getting his shoes wet. But in spite of our differences, Mike and I were best friends for some reason I never figured out. It didn't matter why; we just were.

At the barber shop, two guys named Frank and

Tony gave us haircuts. Neither of the Degans would get a wiffle because they said they made people look like prisoners of war. The wiffle completed my transformation from school to summer, like Clark Kent shedding his suit and necktie to become Superman. Only then would I feel ready for a season of sandlot baseball.

If rain caused a game to be postponed, that never stopped me from fishing at Sailors' Home Pond around the corner and down Rice Road a few houses. In fact, for some reason, the fishing seemed to be better when it was raining. I was told that the City of Quincy stocked the pond with goldfish, catfish and some other fish. Turtles, frogs and snakes were part of the other critters. No matter what the season or weather, there never was a shortage of fun things to do in our neighborhood.

Anyway, the barber used a tube of waxy stuff to make the front of my hair stand up straight, like I'd just seen a ghost in an Abbott and Costello movie at the Wolly. What a place that was. We'd watch two feature films and a cartoon for a quarter. Popcorn or candy cost a nickel. Before people had TV sets the Wolly was the best local entertainment.

Quincy didn't have an organized baseball program at that time for kids my age. Sandlot baseball was the only game in town. There were very few things that made me as happy as our neighborhood baseball games. On most summer days sandlot baseball was my main reason for rolling out of bed in the morning. What also helped me to get up during the summer was the sound of the milkman. Practically every family had one, either from HP Hood or White Brothers. Ours was from Hood, wore a white uniform and cap, and drove a tan step-van with a fold-away seat and sliding doors.

Twice a week he'd stop at the end of our driveway, put a few glass quart bottles of milk into a chicken wire basket, carry them past our garage and around the corner to our back steps. On his return trip to the truck, he'd bring the empty bottles from the previous delivery in the same basket. Sometimes, the empties made enough clanking noise to wake me up on sleepy days. There were times when his whistling did, too, although the only tune I can remember is Happy Days Are Here Again. It must have been his favorite. We could have marked our kitchen wall calendar and set the wall clock by the arrival of the Hood milkman. His visit was one of those repetitive, reassuring routines that seemed to confirm that all was well with the world, at least our corner of it.

If you don't remember those days, milk wasn't homogenized yet, meaning that the cream rose to the top of the glass bottles when they were left standing. If we forgot to take the milk indoors during winter, the contents would expand, sending a column of frozen cream through the top of the bottle. At that time, bottles had cardboard tops that would rise upward with the frozen cream, making it look like the column of cream was wearing a cap.

It wasn't only milk that was delivered. There was a small panel truck that came every Wednesday about the time that I'd be getting home from school. It was brown and tan, with the words, Gentile's Bakery on both sides. That was my favorite delivery because my mother sometimes bought a loaf of cinnamon raisin bread if she had enough spare change. I thought that tasted as good as birthday cake when my mother buttered it.

At the start of summer after 2nd grade, before the sandlot games got started, Scuffy's father said he'd drive all of us to Westland's Sporting Goods store in Quincy Center if our parents would give each of us a dollar to buy a genuine Red Sox baseball cap. The next day was Saturday, and I woke up early to be sure I didn't miss out on getting a cap. When I climbed into the back of Mr. Williams' station wagon, he asked me for my dollar, but I'd forgotten to remind my mother and ran back into the house.

My mother refused to give me the money because she said I'd left a mouthful of milk in my glass at breakfast. I offered to finish it then, but she said it was too late. She dragged me by my hand out of our house and thanked Mr. Williams for his offer and told him that I couldn't go because I was being punished. As hard as I tried not to cry, the tears poured out of me like a waterfall. So, the others left without me and when they got back, they came to the house to show me how great their caps looked, and they did. I was so disgusted that I sulked for the rest of the day, maybe the rest of the summer. I never understood how my mother could be so mean. Her answer was that I had to learn, 'You don't get everything you want in this life.'

As much as I hated both of my parents for nearly scaring me to death at the mental hospital, putting me through surgery at the Carney Hospital and my mother for preventing me from getting a Red Sox cap, I had no choice but to promise my father that I'd try harder to avoid getting into trouble during 3rd grade. To give me more incentive, he said he'd buy me a bicycle the following summer if all went well at school. Now, there was something positive that I could look forward to instead of living in fear of punishment all the time!

Chapter Twenty-two

Uniform #3

A lot had happened during that summer following 2nd grade, but I didn't have time to let it ruin my life because there was so much fun to have in the neighborhood, mostly baseball. Even though I'd never played baseball before moving to Wollaston, I fell in love with the game instantly. We called our team the Red Sox. Boston also had a National League team called the Braves, but my friends and I were Red Sox fans, mostly because of Ted Williams, Boston's superhero. Each of us pretended to be a real Red Sox player but the rule was that nobody was allowed to be Ted because he was so special. I pretended to be Walt Dropo, the rookie first baseman from Moosup, Connecticut.

My friends called me Murph, I played 1st base, and I wore imaginary uniform #3, just like Dropo's number. I thought it was a great number. Some of the neighborhood kids and some of their fathers had shaped the ground to create a pitching mound, home plate, base paths and bases. It was across the sandy road from the cemetery headstones. Even though I was just learning, some of the kids said I was a good player. I couldn't wait to tell that to my brother, Jimmy. Maybe he'd have been proud of me. Who knew? I kept hoping something would make him like me.

The sandy road was a dead-end and the field was practically surrounded by hundreds, maybe thousands of acres of marsh grass interrupted by Black's Creek, Pine Island and countless channels of smelly black muck. Twice a day, the narrow channels filled up with salt water and minnows as the man in the moon saw fit. Black's Creek was hardly the Mississippi River, but the setting still looked to me like a scene from 'The Adventures of Huckleberry Finn' but without the paddle-wheel riverboats. At low tide, the narrow creeks were inhabited mostly by mussels. The star attraction was Black's Creek itself which was long and wide compared to the rest of the marsh. It was hardly the Mighty Mississippi but with a little imagination my mind could turn it into a movie scene from The Adventures of Huckleberry Finn. With a few bales of imaginary cotton and an imaginary paddle-wheel riverboat tied up at the shore of Pine Island it was almost possible to believe I was in Missouri with Tom Sawyer.

Above the marsh was where the dilapidated bridge was that connected the dry land with Pine Island which really wasn't an island at all, it was a peninsula. The floor of the bridge had so many missing and broken boards that you practically had to be a daredevil or an acrobat to avoid falling into the water, six to ten feet below, depending on whether it was high or low tide. Most of us had to hold onto the railings for dear life to keep from falling through the broken pieces. The only exception was Johnny Parker, a short, skinny kid with black hair and dark skin, who lived on Thornton Street. Supposedly, he came from a family of American Indians and a lot of Indians built bridges and skyscrapers because they had excellent balance. That could have been true in Johnny's case because he could cross the bridge by walking on top of the railings without holding on to anything. He looked like one of those tight rope walkers in a circus.

When the tide was high, Black's Creek looked like a great place for a boat ride and, as a matter of fact, there were sailboats tied up at the end of the creek near the Eastern Mass. bus barns, behind Hancock Street, about a mile from Merrymount Beach. The sailboats were used by the Quincy Recreation Department for teaching kids how to sail. Unfortunately, my mother thought sailing was dangerous, so the closest I ever came was to take a ride on a wooden raft.

That happened when Bobby Degan convinced me that building a raft would be great fun. He was the neighborhood kid who came-up with most of the clever ideas. I never knew where he got them, but he thought up some wild stuff. He planned a carnival once in the empty lot behind Mike Dolan's house, the red house on the opposite corner of Dickens Street from us. You couldn't miss the fabulous white birch tree in Mike's front yard and the white post and rail fence surrounding the yard was outstanding. But the white birch wasn't the only spectacular tree in the neighborhood.

Our back yard, just on the other side of Dickens Street, had a sky-high tree called a German Linden. In springtime, it would overflow with yellow buds that dangled from stems like cherries. The tree was about twice as high as our house and when the buds bloomed, the flowers would perfume the air with a fragrance like the Easter Lilies on the upper and lower-level altars at Saint Ann's.

The entire neighborhood would be graced by the sweet aroma of the thousands, maybe millions, of delicate cream-colored blossoms. When that tree was in full-bloom, and the breeze was coming off the bay, people could smell the German Linden flowers from as far away as Marlboro Street which, according to my father, was a quarter mile away heading toward Wollaston Center. The Beechwood Knoll was like the Garden of Eden compared to our neighborhood in Park Ridge which had mostly grass and shrubs populating the flattest land I'd ever seen. I'd heard somebody say that you could go 1,000 miles south of Lake Michigan before you came to the first hill. While that probably wasn't true, in Quincy and some of the surrounding towns, there were plenty of hills, practically everywhere.

Bobby Degan's raft was pretty exciting but other

than the Degans, I was the only one willing to ride on the thing. Bobby had designed it and we all helped nail the boards together. Bobby was clever, smart and excellent at figuring-out ways to do things. He could have become the next Phineas T. Barnum, the circus genius who created the travelling 'tails on rails' concept. Maybe he would someday do something high-tech for all I knew, something like inventing the personal computer and revolutionizing our way of life.

Anyway, Bobby's raft idea nearly turned into a disaster. Donny, Bobby and I didn't know how quickly the tide flowed out once the direction reversed. Or that the poles we cut to be used to steer the raft would get stuck in the soft muck at the bottom of the creek. After we lost the poles, the raft was on its own and we had no way to steer it. As it headed for the rapids beneath Merrymount Bridge, it was gaining speed like a toboggan heading down the tall slope at the Furnace Brook Golf Club on Wollaston Hill. Salt water was washing over the raft by the bucketful. As brave as I thought I was, the ride got pretty scary when the raft began to spin in a slow circle in the current and I started getting dizzy. I knew that my mother would go berserk if I fell in, especially if I got muck on my shoes or drowned! Yikes!

I was praying like mad that we'd strike land before the raft reached the rapids that flowed beneath the green metal railings of the Merrymount Bridge. Luckily, we did when a corner of the raft struck a clump of grass jutting into the creek. We were able to safely jump to land before we wound up lost at sea, waiting to be rescued by the crew of some tramp steamer on its way back from Africa. That episode taught me that seeing a movie about a riverboat hadn't qualified us to navigate Black's Creek on a rickety, rolling raft. What were we thinking? It also taught me that there is power in prayer sometimes because that's what I'd been doing as the rapids kept getting closer.

Chapter Twenty-three

Other skeletons

Black's Creek was visible from the baseball field, but not the other way around. I'd walked through the cemetery beside the dirt road only once because I thought walking over dead guys was pretty spooky and it gave me the creeps. If that wasn't reason enough, the Degans told me about the skeleton that got loose once – during a hurricane in 1938 – and it was still wandering through the marsh somewhere, seeking to create mayhem. They pointed out places where the grass had been recently stepped on and flattened by the skeleton. They also told me that if I listened hard enough, I could hear other skeletons scratching at the inside of their coffins, trying to get out.

The Degans always had some horror story, like the one about quicksand somewhere in the marsh and about some kids from North Quincy who stumbled into it and never returned. According to Donny, the quicksand swallowed them up. But Bobby maintained that they were probably captured by the wandering skeleton who might have eaten them. Sometimes I'd have trouble getting to sleep thinking about those ghost stories.

During summer, I lived for baseball and the homemade field was my favorite place. It was on the right side of the dirt road at the marsh end of Andrews Road. There was never an exact time for a game to begin; the starting time was whenever enough of us showed up, which meant when we had finished our chores. Chores were a part of every kid's life, and most parents were strict about them. If your chores weren't finished, you weren't likely to play any baseball or have any other fun and that's all there was to it at my house.

If I was getting set to head to the field from home and somebody else was heading that way, he'd probably shout, 'Game's on, Murph, I'll beat you there,' and we'd both run all the way. At other times, you'd have thought we were using smoke signals to let everyone know we were ready to play ball because kids would show up at the same time. It was almost magical.

Being at the field meant that my chores were behind me for a while as was my mother's nagging and me getting picked on by my brother and sisters. Because my father needed his car for work, my mother had no way to get to the field to bring me home. I was as safe at that field as if I was stealing home plate on a wild pitch and the ball rolled down a rabbit hole. Even if I hadn't loved baseball, not worrying about my mother showing up made the field a wonderful place to be. It was the closest place that I knew to a paradise.

Speaking of the family car, my father drove it around New England selling dental equipment; my mother used to say that he loved Ritter dental equipment more than her. Knowing my father, she might have been right and, knowing my mother, I would have understood why. It seemed as though the visitors who came to our house were usually men from the dental business instead of normal people, usually asking my father to draw office plans for some dentist. At our supper table, the dental business was what my father wanted to talk about more than what was going on with the rest of us. Sometimes, especially on Saturdays, he'd drag me around to dental equipment showrooms and to construction sites where there were wires and pipes being installed for the equipment. Was that ever torture for me, and I made a firm decision about my career path then – I was never going to do anything involving dental offices or dental equipment. Oh my gosh, was that boring!

Anyway, the ballfield was a baseball fantasy land and sometimes I hated leaving there, even when I'd get hungry. I'd rather eat the giant blackberries from the thorny bushes that grew beneath the climb-up-and-sit pine trees. Those trees had the best view of Quincy Bay and the row of islands that separated the bay from Boston Harbor. My mother would be furious when I'd come home with pine sap on my pants or marsh muck on my shoes. I can remember her trying to remove the pine sap with nail polish remover and turpentine, all the while yelling at me.

Wollaston Beach was just a few minutes' walk from the baseball field and it ranked as my next favorite place. The beach end of Fenno Street led directly to it. There was a panoramic view of it from the adjacent pine trees and one of the Boston skylines from up there also. Even at low tide there were interesting things to see on the beach like washed-up jelly fish, horseshoe crabs stranded within the rocky sea wall, clams burrowed into the mud, and pieces of colored glass polished smooth by the repeated churning of the tide. There were times when I'd just sit on the wall and watch sailboats drifting by, especially during Quincy Bay race week.

Other times, I'd hunt for flat skipping stones to scale across the top of the water when the tide came in and there were no waves. Among my friends, I held the record for the second most skips – eleven. Bobby Degan held position #1, as he did for everything else. It wasn't that he was so much better than the rest of us; he just refused to lose at anything. That's what my mother was like when she joined into my father's poker games in the basement of the house in Park Ridge. She wasn't any better than his men friends; she just refused to lose. Boy, did it drive him crazy when she won.

There were two yacht clubs along the stretch of beach closer to Dorchester – Wollaston Yacht Club and Squantum Yacht Club. Scores of boats were moored close by and at busy times it was fascinating to watch the sailboats coming and going. Sometimes, usually weekend nights, there'd be parties and dances there with music drifting across the bay and the echoes of laughter and adult voices engaged in lively conversations. I didn't know anybody who owned a boat or anyone who belonged to either yacht club, so I had no reason to go there. But since I was accustomed to feeling left out at home, I didn't pay much attention to not being included in the yacht club activities.

Each of the buildings was built on wooden posts big as telephone poles and connected to shore by a wooden walkway with railings. Seeing the buildings at high tide made them look like they were floating on the water. It was another interesting part of the beach scene, another interesting part of our neighborhood and another interesting part of Quincy. How lucky I was to have moved there from Park Ridge where there was nothing interesting for a kid to do.

Who ever heard of a neighborhood like the Beechwood Knoll? A beach with yacht clubs, boat races, a creek, an island, a bridge, marshland, a fishing hole and a baseball field? It was unbelievable. It was like living in a fairyland, almost too good to believe. But nothing was as exciting to me as the baseball field. That was the best part of the entire cross-country move for me, no doubt about it. My family had moved from Illinois to paradise, and I got to play baseball in paradise, all summer long, weather permitting.

That doesn't even take into consideration the nearby places where my friends and I could go. But most of that was to come later, assuming I could stay out of trouble during 3rd grade. If my father bought me a bike, I would be able to go to the Naval Air Station which was at the Boston end of the beach. The kids in our neighborhood talked about how much fun it was to watch the Navy planes taking off and landing.

The adjacent neighborhood to the air station was named Squantum which was on a hilly peninsula that led to the Long Island bridge that was connected to a chain of islands that separated Quincy Bay from the Atlantic Ocean. Supposedly there were fun things to do there too including watching large ships heading into and out of the harbor. I was enthused that I'd be able to do more of those things after I got a bike.

Chapter Twenty-four

No nonsense

When I started 3rd grade my teacher was Miss Pebbler, who was known for saying, 'In this classroom there'll be no nonsense,' and 'I'll have no nonsense.' She demanded respect from everyone in her class and she got it. She was the kind of person that was likely to stand in the way of me getting a bike at the end of the school year if I caused any trouble. She was large enough to be physically intimidating and I was very careful to be on my best behavior.

I must have been pretty near perfect, because I don't remember a single incident of me causing trouble. The only issue was Miss Pebbler told my parents at every PTA meeting that I was 'under-achieving.' That was better than being labeled a troublemaker, but my father said I'd still have to work harder if I wanted a bike. Other than that, 3rd grade was smooth sailing, as the saying went.

By springtime, I was daydreaming about baseball and asking everyone I knew if the Red Sox had any good, new players. I also was curious about the Braves because I read on a sports page that the Braves might win the National League pennant in the upcoming season. They supposedly had some excellent well-known players, like Alvin Dark and Eddie Stanky. Those were players I'd heard about who were good players. The Braves also had two excellent pitchers named Warren Spahn and Johny Sain. I decided to start collecting Braves trading cards as well as Red Sox ones. Anyway, the Braves uniforms were much better looking and much more colorful.

My mother came from a large family. Even though I never met all of her siblings, she used to recite all their names along with hers, and the list got stuck in my head from hearing it so often. There was Katie, Connie, Molly, Maudie, Johnny, Butcher, Eddie and Adelaide. I never met my mother's parents because her father died when she was two and her mother died nine years before I was born. Similarly, my father's parents both passed on before I was born, meaning I never knew what it was like to have a grandparent of any kind.

As to my mother's three brothers – Johnny, Butcher and Eddie – she said that Butch had been a local hero when he played semi-pro ball around Boston and was invited to spring training one year for a try-out with the

Braves. He was a left-handed, power-hitting first baseman. I had a chance to ask him if he thought the Braves were going to be any good that year. His answer was that they could win the pennant if they had another good pitcher. But, because Spahn and Sain were the only good ones, there was a saying that went, 'Spahn and Sain and pray for rain.' That meant that Spahn and Sain could probably win two games of most three-game series but, after that, the fans would need to pray for rain so that the third game would be postponed until another date when Spahn or Sain might be available to pitch. Otherwise, the team would probably lose most of the third games.

One of the strangest things about my mother was that she seemed to be a different person when other people would stop by our house. When she had visitors, she would be happy, light-hearted and talk about things I didn't think she knew anything about. Otherwise, I never heard her talking about current news events like sports or politics or movies or anything interesting, but visitors seemed to bring out the best in her.

While my mother's brothers were visiting our house one day, they were discussing the Red Sox and the Braves with my mother. I thought there was something wrong with my hearing because my uncles were acting like my mother knew what they were talking about, including a comment she made about a pitcher for the Cleveland Indians named Bob Feller. She said that he could throw a fastball 103 miles per hour. When I asked her how she knew so much about baseball, she said she'd been a tomboy when she was growing up and had played a lot of baseball. Her brother, Eddie, said that she was a better player than he was, which I thought was a joke. But Johnny and Butch said it was true.

I remember asking her what position she played, figuring she wouldn't know the names of any positions. Her answer was, 'All of them, mostly pitcher and shortstop.' I wasn't born yesterday, and I knew that those positions were the ones played by the best players. Ha! That certainly couldn't have been my mother... or could it? On a boys' team no less. I was still pretty sure she was pulling my leg until she sent me upstairs to get my glove, Jimmy's glove and a ball so we could have a catch in the back yard. When I realized that she was serious, you could have knocked me over with a feather! If my mother turned out to be any good, it would be a miracle, or so I thought.

After shedding her apron, she grabbed the ball from me, tucked Jimmy's Rawlings glove under her left arm, spit into her hands one at a time, and rubbed up the ball. She put Jimmy's glove on her left hand, held the ball with her right, paced across the yard, turned to face me and announced, 'Sixty feet, six inches. Batter up!' What the heck? That actually was the correct, Major League Baseball distance from the pitching mound rubber to home plate. But this was my mother, Adelaide Murphy, not a professional baseball pitcher. Then she used the toe of her right foot to 'paw' at the dirt like a real pitcher would do. Johnny shouted, 'Show the kid your fastball, Ad, but don't hurt him.'

They all started laughing but I was already too nervous to laugh. She went into a full windup and I couldn't believe what I was seeing – she was about to throw me a fastball as I got into a crouch. In addition to becoming scared for my life, I realized that Jimmy might beat the crap out of me for letting her use his glove and ball.

That glove was always shined up, like his Florsheim shoes. It shined like the hood on my father's Buick. Jimmy called it a spit shine and I'd watched him rub brown Kiwi shoe polish on it many times. Then he'd buff it with a shoe brush and rub it with a shoe rag. He cared more about that glove than anything else he owned... anything!

Then she did it – she threw me a pitch that set the palm of my left hand on fire when I caught it, right where my index finger joins my middle one. My hand felt like I'd grabbed a hot potato from the oven and, if you've ever done that, you know how much my hand hurt. When I played ball at the neighborhood field, I'd had balls thrown to me by the other guys that would sting my glove hand, but my mother's pitch felt like a sting on steroids. Somehow, until she threw it, I was still believing she'd throw me a soft, girly pitch but not so; she threw me a Bob Feller bolt of lightning.

Her fastball looked faster than the ones my brother threw, and I walked into our house so nobody would see me hopping around in pain. My hand started to swell immediately, and I ran it under cold water at the kitchen sink. I felt like the village idiot. Imagine a woman, my mother no less, injuring me with a pitch. After that, I had a different opinion of who and what she was. Hmmm – my mother, the baseball player!

That was something about her that I admired.

I wondered where she'd been hiding this other person, this baseball player who was good enough to play on a boys' team. Why hadn't I ever seen her before? When I thought more about it, I realized it was somewhat the same with my father. He was so serious most of the time that it was scary being around him. But I admired him when dental salesmen and dentists came to our house and praised him for dental office plans, he'd drawn, or members of AA visited him and praised him for a talk he'd given at an AA meeting somewhere. To me, he seemed like a different person at those times.

There was still no doubt in my mind that both of my parents were grouches so I was still careful not to get too close to them. But I was beginning to appreciate some of their better qualities, and they seemed to be changing their feelings about me, at least temporarily.

Chapter Twenty-five

Parental power

The summer following 3rd grade produced two of the most memorable events in my childhood. As he had promised, Big Jim Murphy told me we were going to look at bicycles on the first Saturday morning after classes ended. I couldn't remember ever being that excited. We headed to Quincy Center to the Firestone store, which was a place that sold, installed and repaired auto tires. I had no idea why we were going there until my father took me inside where there was a bicycle department. But the bikes there were American bikes and I'd been dreaming about an English racing bike.

When I told my father that they weren't the style of bike I wanted, he gave me a lecture about having a patriotic duty to buy an American bike and not buy one that was made somewhere else. The deal was that I had to pick out one of the clunky-looking Firestone bikes or go without a bike. Period! Well, that was a lousy choice if there ever was one and it was clear that he had parental power and I had no power.

Before I'd had a chance to compare the bikes, my father asked a salesman to explain the differences between the models that were on the display floor. I already knew I didn't want any of them. To me, they looked like girls' bikes, and they had goofy accessories like headlights, shock absorber springs, foot brakes, rearview mirrors, horns, book carriers and other things that looked silly. It seemed more like equipment for autos than bikes.

Some of the neighborhood kids with bikes had the right kind – racing bikes with hand brakes, three-speed shifters and narrow tires. That was exactly what I wanted. What was the big deal about where it was made? The Firestone bikes looked like they'd been designed by someone with no taste whatsoever. What was my father doing? I reasoned that he wouldn't be caught dead riding a bike that looked like one of the Firestone bikes if he was a kid like me. I'd learn later that my father had never owned a bike himself, so he had nothing to compare with the Firestone bikes. Those bikes even had whitewall tires, which were just wrong, all wrong compared to what I'd been dreaming about.

Needless to say, we left the store with the bike my father liked best, a red one with twenty-six-inch wheels and most of the clunk junk, including shock absorber springs. When we got it home, it took my father about a half hour to open the cardboard boxes and assemble the bike. My friends stopped by to watch. I had to admit that it didn't look so bad – what could be bad about a shiny, red bike that could take me everywhere I wanted to go?

My father acted like he was proud of the bike, and I believed that he thought that it was better than what I had wanted. I spent most of that Saturday riding with the other kids. We went as far as Quincy Center and made the trip in about a quarter of the time it usually took to walk, which was very cool. The whole experience made me feel closer to my father and there hadn't been many of those events before that. Looking back, it may have been one of the few times when I felt like my father cared about me and that was a special feeling.

As though not wanting to be outdone by my father, my mother came up with a brilliant idea of her own – setting up a Kool-Aid stand at the bus stop. She actually offered to buy a cannister of Kool-Aid powder, mix it with water and add ice cubes so that our neighbors, coming home from work, could have a cold drink when they got off the hot bus. She made a cardboard sign, on which she printed 'Kool-Aid 5 cents.' Whose mother was this? Mine had never been this helpful.

When people got off the bus from Ashmont, I'd be right there, with my parents' folding card table, paper cups and a pitcher of cold lemon Kool-Aid with ice. Busses didn't have air conditioning in those days, so the Kool-Aid was a great idea. I quickly realized that some people drank a cupful without first asking the price, so it was too late for them to argue when I told them it was a dime. Meanwhile others asked the price first and I told them it was a nickel so I wouldn't lose the sale. My mother had a saying – 'Half a loaf is better than no bread,' – which seemed to apply. I quickly ditched my mother's sign.

'That's stealing!' my mother bellowed like she was the Mount Vesuvius volcano. According to her, I had cheated our neighbors. She yanked on my right ear and ordered me to go to everyone's house who'd paid a dime and return a nickel to them. Worse than that, she followed me around the neighborhood to make sure I spoke with everyone and if I couldn't remember who they were, I was told to ask each one of them. So, my business was shut down after only one day. That was more like the Adelaide Murphy that I knew. As usual, it was another case of my mother embarrassing me publicly!

Of course, my mother, the model of Catholic decency, couldn't leave the issue there. She demanded that I pay a Saturday afternoon visit to St. Ann's to pour out my soul in a Confession booth. She insisted, when I got home, that I tell her which priest had heard my Confession and whether he'd concluded that cheating our neighbors was a mortal sin or a venial sin. She also wanted to know what penance he'd ordered me to complete; penance meaning to say a specific number of specific prayers at the altar rail to receive forgiveness. What the heck? I was told that if I failed to say my penance and to recite 'a good act of contrition,' I'd go to hell. I definitely didn't want to end up in hell. Who would?

I'd always had difficulty remembering the prayer of contrition, mostly because the language sounded like it had been written during the Middle Ages by a monk in a cave in the Italian Alps. I used to wonder why I couldn't just say to the priest that I was sorry for all the bad stuff I had done. Something like, 'Sorry I did all that stuff, father, and I'll try to do better.' And what was it with all the 'thees' and 'thous' in the prayer? There was too much hullabaloo for my liking and the reason I went to Confession was that I was ordered to go, like most of my friends.

What compounded the problem between me and Confession was the scary stuff my mother had drilled into my head. It was that fire and brimstone preaching about God's wrath. According to her, God might harm my family because of bad things I did. Like what? Like my father might 'fall off the wagon' and start drinking again or might be killed in a plane crash or a car accident because I was a bad person. I had to listen to those threats frequently. Maybe I believed her threats because the Sunday gospel readings at Mass had stories from the Bible about people being tortured, slain or turned into pillars of salt. It was a simple message – do good and be rewarded; do bad and be punished. Somehow, with my mother, the bad always seemed to outweigh the good. As a result, my life had more shame than pride, more guilt than glory, more fear than comfort.

Confession marked the low point of every Catholic boy's life in our neighborhood. It was held on Saturday afternoon in the lower church, where there were three Confession booths, those private compartments that looked something like phone booths except there was no glass. Each one held three people – a priest in the middle section behind a door and a person in the section on each side of him behind a curtain that faced the church. A panel with a screen and a sliding partition separated the priest from each confessor. The priest sat on a chair while the confessors knelt on a kneeler. After hearing each Confession, the priest told each person how many prayers of contrition to say.

On a typical Saturday, there were two priests hearing Confession, one of them was frequently the pastor. I always tried to avoid the pastor because he was such a grouch. The regular priests, Father Daily and Father Duffy, who were called curates, were younger and easier to talk with. That was good for me because I hated getting yelled at by the pastor, who was named Monsignor Walter Leach. He was about sixty whereas the curates were in their twenties. For me, it was much scarier going to Confession with Msgr.

Leach than with Fr. Daily or Fr. Duffy.

My sister, Barbara, told me she never minded going to confession because she never did bad things. Ha! What planet was she living on? How about the times when she pushed me around or shoved me through the thin ice at the pond? And refused to talk to me or to share her candy with me? How about the times when I'd have to stay in the house until the four of us kids had all finished our chores and Barbara took her sweet time doing hers, causing me to miss going fishing or be late for playing baseball? But she wasn't the only one who pretended to be perfect. I'd never seen anyone else in the family go to Confession. I concluded that I was the only bad banana in the bunch, which was consistent with how my mother made me feel.

Chapter Twenty-Six

'Killer'

The name Walter was intimidating to me because the heavyweight wrestling champion was named Walter 'Killer' Kowalski. I'd seen him in news films at the Wolly in which he seemed to be the toughest, meanest, dirtiest wrestler on the planet. This guy did the wildest, craziest things I'd ever seen, including trying to gouge out his opponent's eyeballs and biting off the other guy's ears. Although my father said the sport was rehearsed and the wrestlers were actors, it all looked pretty real to me and Kowalski looked more like a killer than a wrestler, especially when his opponent started to bleed from his injuries! That to me was definitely real!

The pastor at St. Ann's was another Walter – Monsignor Walter Leach. He was tall, thin and seemed to look suspiciously at people, like he was an FBI agent. My father didn't trust the FBI because he thought its director, J. Edgar Hoover, was actually a criminal. So being an FBI agent might make someone a bad person in my father's mind. Oddly enough, that was how he felt about the pastor too, something to do with trying to embarrass parishioners into giving the church their 'hard-earned' money. What really annoyed my father was when the pastor decided to read from the pulpit during Mass the names of parishioners who were not paying the amount of money to the church that the pastor had assigned. My father blew his top over that! He threatened to go to a different church if the pastor ever read his name out loud.

Monsignor Leach had a half-ring of white hair on the back and sides of his head, from one ear to the other, and only a single strand of hair on top, like it was a keepsake from his youth. The guy was so somber that he could have been the person who administered electric shock treatments to the patients at the insane asylum at Mattapan – the nuthouse! Worse than that, he might have been the one who performed frontal lobotomies on the hopeless patients. My father used to say that in cowboy movies – my father's favorite entertainment – the bad guys wore black clothing and black hats while the good guys wore white clothing and white hats. The pastor wore a black uniform and a black hat, which made me think that my father might have been right about him being a bad guy.

My father had a friend from AA, a lawyer, who had a deep, round scar in his forehead from a frontal lobotomy. I took a close look at him once when he was sitting on the sofa in our living room. He looked like someone had drilled a hole at the top right center of his forehead, about the size of a quarter. It was some of these circumstances that shaded my opinion of the pastor. So, when I went to Confession, my first move was to see if and where the pastor was located so that I could be sure to avoid him. If he was there waiting in a booth, the confessional door would have his nameplate posted. But it really wasn't necessary to look for it because there would be hardly anyone sitting in the pews in front of his booth – only daring people and people like my sister Barbara would take that risk. He had a reputation for yelling at kids if he didn't like something they said or how they said it.

As soon as I spied the dreaded nameplate, I walked to the other occupied booth to avoid him. However, I hadn't escaped him at all because the next thing I knew, the pastor was standing beside the pew where I was seated. He was ordering people to come to his booth, and I was one of those he pointed at. Egad, that drove fear into my heart like he'd stabbed me with a pitchfork. After all, my mother had warned me that I could be excommunicated from the Catholic Church for having cheated our neighbors. I was instantly terrified, broke into a sweat, started shaking, got a case of weak knees and my Adam's apple began to quiver. If anybody was going to expel me from the church, it would definitely be Msgr. Leach and since he'd already seen me eyeball to eyeball, I couldn't think of any way to escape my fate.

When I entered the narrow, darkened booth and knelt down, I began shaking like I was inside an Eskimo igloo or inside our basement meat freezer, the one that looked like a white coffin and was located across from my father's tool bench. When the pastor opened the partition and questioned me through the screen, I must have sounded like my mother's warbled imitation of the boogeyman. I couldn't believe that I started to cry. I was nearly nine years old and thought I was too tough to cry. A lot I knew! Monsignor Leach instructed me to calm down and told me things probably were not as bad as I thought. That didn't sound like anything the pastor might say. Was I in the wrong booth or what?

When I was finally able to choke the words out about how I raised the price of the Kool-Aid, Monsignor Leach burst out laughing... Cub Scouts honor, that's what he really did! I'm sure that everybody in the church heard him and maybe people outside on Hancock Street. When I asked him what kind of sin I had committed, he said he wasn't sure if I had committed any and added, 'Someday you're going to make a great businessman, kid.' He asked me to tell him my name and made me promise that I'd look him up when I got older so that he could buy some stock in my company. What the heck? I didn't even know what stock was until I asked my father about it later at supper.

When I heard the explanation about how people buy stock, it sounded like a gambling scheme, like betting on horses like my brother used to do. Jimmy liked to go to a racetrack in East Boston called Suffolk Downs. I remember my father telling Jimmy that betting was for losers, and he'd never get ahead in life by 'playing the ponies.' I wondered if the pastor also bet on horses. I got confused trying to understand how business and betting differed. Of course, most of the kids I knew were just as confused about what was mortal sin, venial sin and no sin.

Nevertheless, I was a new person when I left St. Ann's that Saturday afternoon because Monsignor Leach – old grouchy Monsignor Leach – had opened my eyes about sin and punishment. The next question in my mind was could my mother be wrong about the other parts of Catholicism and if I was living under the daily fear of God's wrath for no good reason. By then I had realized that I'd never seen either of my parents go to Confession or to Communion. Maybe my mother had been making up the rules she used to drill into my head day after day, rules that my friends had never heard about. God must have known my mother wasn't perfect; even I knew it. So, when she made mistakes or did mean things, why didn't she go to Confession?

I asked her about that once and she told me that she never committed any sins and that was true for my father, also. But I wasn't buying that explanation. If she was such a perfect parent, why did she yell at me, lie to me, play dirty tricks on me, break my favorite toy, scare me half to death with threats about the nuthouse, tell a doctor to cut me up, and abandon me twice? I'd have loved to hear her answers to those questions but was afraid to ask. I knew if I asked my father about some of those questions, he would have blown a gasket, yelled at me and supported everything my mother had done as having had my best interest at heart. There was no winning.

How could I have doubted my father's behavior anyway, knowing that he'd bought me a bike a few weeks earlier? Getting a bicycle had proven to be a passage from childhood to adolescence and I didn't want to disappoint my father by acting like I suspected that he wasn't a good person. I did, however, tell him what Monsignor Leach had said about me overcharging the neighbors for Kool-Aid and found-out it was the first my father had heard about the situation. Why hadn't my mother discussed it with him if what I did was so terrible?

So, I asked my father why the pastor didn't think I'd committed some kind of sin by overcharging the neighbors although my mother had gone crazy about it. My father knew better than to criticize her, so he gave me one of his politically correct answers. I could tell that he was aggravated about how she had handled the situation, but he wasn't about to criticize her to me. In some ways, my family life was like a conspiracy – my two parents were united in their opposition to me as were my three siblings.

As to the Kool-Aid caper, my father suggested that I read the rules of the Catholic Church, aka the Baltimore Catechism, about sin, to figure out the answer to my own question. I knew that would be a wild goose chase because there wouldn't be anything about selling Kool-Aid in the catechism and he was just trying to avoid any conflict between my mother and him. I'd learned long ago that there was no resolution to those issues... life just went on.

Chapter Twenty-seven

Coconut Grove

Shortly before 4th grade began, my mother rode the bus home from Ashmont Station with Mrs. Reddington, who lived on Dickens Street, four houses beyond ours. My mother was coming home from a 'back to school' clothes shopping trip to Boston and Mrs. Reddington was coming home from her job at a downtown Boston department store.

I remembered Mrs. Reddington well for three reasons. First, she was a short, plump woman who was so overweight that she wobbled from one side to the other when she walked. Second, her husband had died recently, and the wake was held in the living room of their house. I didn't know that was possible; I thought everyone had to be buried from a funeral home. Third, she was always talkative and pleasant whenever she passed by our house if I was in the yard. Not many people in the neighborhood were friendly and I liked her because she was.

Mrs. Reddington had a nephew named Georgie O'Brien who had been orphaned six years earlier as the result of a notorious Boston fire at a night club called the Coconut Grove. I had no idea where he lived before 1948 but that was the year when he moved into Mrs. Reddington's house in our neighborhood. Mrs. Reddington asked my mother if I could introduce Georgie to the other kids in the neighborhood and, because I was a year older, show him around school when it opened. My mother was always glad to volunteer me to do good deeds, as she called them.

It was easy for me to like Georgie because he was a devoted Red Sox fan. Also, because he was an excellent baseball player and because he fitted right in with the sandlot team. He was a year younger than me, but big for his age, strong for his size, was the only kid in the neighborhood with curly hair and he liked baseball as much as I did. The only drawback to the arrangement was that I wouldn't be able to ride my bike to school because my father had prohibited me from giving anyone else a ride on the bike. I would have to continue to walk to school as in the previous two years.

When 4th grade started for me, I felt like I'd already ridden the bike 500 miles since my father bought it in June. Although he had made a big deal about how much better it was than foreign made bikes, the Firestone bike had a problem by the time school started

– rust. The chrome shock absorbers on both sides of the steering fork had rusted and sometimes they locked in one position when I went over a bump or off of a curb stone. That would cause the front tire to jam against the front fender, stopping the bike instantly, like a galloping horse balking at a hurdle. I had mentioned the problem to my father, but he hadn't done anything to correct the problem yet. When I'd be riding, I had to make sure that I hung on to the handlebars for dear life or I might have been thrown over them and landed on the pavement headfirst. So much for my father's belief that American products were always better!

My mother had made it clear that I was responsible for Georgie being on time for school every day, no excuses allowed. But on the very first day, Georgie was ten minutes late getting to my house. My father had left the house earlier, my mother had taken the bus to Ashmont and there was only one way to get to school on time – the bike! I had to decide whether to break my promise to my father or the one I'd made to my mother. That was like choosing between wrestling a grizzly bear or a crocodile.

So off we went on that Monday morning, with Georgie perched on the handlebars. Out of my driveway, down the Havilend Street hill, right turn around the corner onto Rice Road and directly into the pothole that I couldn't see because Georgie was blocking my vision. I knew the hole was there somewhere, but I was rushing to get to school on time and had forgotten exactly where the darned thing was located. The front wheel hit the rim of the hole so hard

that it felt like I had gone over the edge of the Grand Canyon and slammed into a stone wall. The rusted shock absorbers locked in the closed position, causing the front wheel to freeze as rigidly as if someone had stuck a broom stick through the spokes. Suddenly, Georgie and I were launched over the handlebars, like a pair of synchronized Olympic high divers or members of the Flying Wallendas circus act without a safety net. We landed hard, Georgie on his butt and me on my head.

I was told later that Georgie had only minor scrapes and bruises. But me? I was unconscious like I'd been knocked out by Joe Louis, the heavyweight boxing champion of the world. An ambulance took me to the Quincy City Hospital, where I was diagnosed with having a concussion and I spent five days there. The best parts were that I got to miss five days of school and nobody at the hospital yelled at me, not even once. I could walk to the kitchen to get ice cream whenever I wanted, and people served me my meals in bed. It was great! I didn't have any worries except how badly my bike was damaged and whether I'd be able to ride it again.

It was Friday when I was discharged and sent home. My parents never yelled at me about the accident, but my father had a few choice words like, 'Maybe landing on your head knocked some sense into it.' Mrs. Reddington blamed me for the accident and told Georgie to stay away from me. How was the accident my fault? If he'd gotten to my house on time, we wouldn't have had to use the bike in the first place.

But, of course, he never told his aunt that he was late. The front wheel of the bike was bent so far out of shape that it was useless, not to mention the damage to the front fender, handlebars and other parts. The Firestone bike turned out to be a pile of junk; even my father had to agree with that.

My teacher that year was Mrs. Hanlon, and she was beautiful. Her first name was Mary and I thought that she was the prettiest woman I'd ever met. I was determined to do well that year because I wanted her to like me as much as I liked her. That was all the motivation I needed to stay out of trouble. At the first conference she had with my parents, she told them that I was a good student and well behaved. My father told me if I kept up the good work, he'd think about buying me another bike when the school year was over.

Soon after the pothole disaster, the city sent a dump truck with two workers to fill in the canyon and I remember watching the two of them, both with potbellies and soiled white T-shirts, making the repairs. One T-shirt was blank and worn by a guy with a brown fedora hat that was pretty worn-out looking. He had a pack of matches stuck into his hat band. He had somehow wrapped the left sleeve of his T-shirt around a pack of Lucky Strike cigarettes at his shoulder, probably because his shirt didn't have a pocket. Identifying his brand of smokes was easy because the Lucky Strike package was white with a red bullseye in the center. I even remember that packs of Luckies had letters on the sides that stood for 'Lucky Strike means fine tobacco.' In those days, men were identified by whether they were smokers or not, and if so, what brand they smoked.

The other worker had a brown faded football printed on the front of his shirt with the words, 'Boston Yanks.' The Yanks were a National Football League franchise, and the team played its home games at Fenway Park. He wore a black baseball cap with the logo of the New York Yankees in white letters. Funny how two guys, a truck, a pile of asphalt, a roller, some shovels and rakes can provide entertainment for kids. You'd have thought they were building a skyscraper.

My father, when I told him about the road repairs, called the workers 'professional potbellied pothole people.' He used to like twisting words around like that. And, when I asked him what the letters DPW meant that were on the doors of the white, dump truck, my father grinned and said, 'Diggers and pothole workers.' Later, I found-out they stood for Department of Public Works. At least my father had a sense of humor once in a while. The truck doors each had the official seal of the city with some letters, numbers and a scene with sailing ships and a pine tree as I remember. We watched the whole procedure until one of the workers rolled the new asphalt level with the surrounding road surface and the other worker put the tools into the back of the truck.

I had watched something similar about three months earlier at Mount Wollaston Cemetery when some guys with a similar truck were burying a coffin. My friends and I sat on a wall behind the grave and talked to each other about where heaven and hell were and how anyone got there from Quincy. Later, I thought, as a joke, that I should have said, 'You get to heaven at the airport, but you take a subway if you're going to hell.' One of us said he didn't believe people went anywhere when they died. It might have been Baldy. Then we started singing the 'Worm song.' That's the one about corpses that goes:

The worms crawl in, the worms crawl out,
The worms play pinochle on your snout.
And one little worm who's very shy,
Crawls in your ear and out your eye.

We all laughed, jumped on our bikes and took off for who knows where. At our ages we always were wondering about confusing things like death. I had heard something about a flying saucer that was supposed to have crashed in New Mexico and some of us wondered about who was flying the thing and if it came from heaven. Mike Dolan said he was planning to be a priest someday, so he usually wanted to discuss life's mysteries about angels, how babies were born and how people died but nobody else cared very much. His brain was wired differently than mine. He wanted to talk about all the details. My sisters told me that mothers delivered babies, not storks and that was good enough for me. If Mike thought I needed to know anymore he was just plain wrong. But he was the only kid I could share my thoughts with, even though I never wanted to hear all of his screwy thoughts about babies, girls, death and flying saucers. I would never have guessed that Mike would actually become a priest someday. Sometimes life is filled with surprises.

Chapter Twenty-eight

Open wide

When I was in 4th grade, our family dentist, Dr. Burrell, found a cavity in one of my teeth while he was cleaning them. Dr. Burrell reminded me of Dr. Dalton, the surgeon who had operated on me at the Carney Hospital. He was a tall, older man with white hair and eyeglasses. He kept saying, 'Open wide,' while he was cleaning my teeth and before long my jaw was killing me. His assistant called my mother to make an appointment for me to get a filling and a week or two later I went back to his office to have it done. Barbara told me that getting a filling would hurt a lot, but my father said there was some kind of a 'shot' from a needle that would take the pain away. Dorothy told me to pretend that I was going to the dentist but go somewhere else instead. I knew my parents wouldn't fall for that trick.

So, a couple of weeks later I found myself climbing the staircase with the black and white linoleum tiles to Dr. Burrell's office, which was above the Blackwood Pharmacy at the corner of Hancock and Beale Streets. I kept thinking about what Barbara said about how much drilling my tooth would hurt me and what my father said about getting a needle stuck in my gums. I was pretty scared about having another bad experience with a doctor.

Dr. Burrell was standing next to the dental chair, wearing a white smock, and his assistant was wearing a white uniform dress. It was a hot day and both of them were sweating even though there was a fan operating in the room. They both looked pretty old to me and looked terribly serious while they were getting ready to drill my tooth.

I studied the office layout and everything they were doing, to make sure I had an escape route just in case I couldn't stand the pain. I had learned my lesson at the Carney Hospital, to escape while you've still got the chance when necessary. When Dr. Burrell reached for the chrome drill that was hanging from a stand next to the dental chair, I saw him put a pointed thing like a nail into it and start the drill spinning. I noticed that a black belt that spun the drill made a whirring sound I didn't remember hearing the last time I was there. The dentist said, 'Open wide,' again and added, 'this won't hurt much.' Much? I didn't want it to hurt at all!

Then he told the assistant to hold me down. I don't remember her name, but I do remember that she was a big woman, built like a wrestler, or a football player and she smelled of body odor or, as my mother called it, B.O. I hated that smell; it made my eyes water. It reminded me of my mother's enforcement of my personal hygiene habits, regularly inspecting my fingernails, hands, elbows, neck, ears, face and teeth before I'd leave for school. She couldn't let it go at that, though. Anytime I'd have friends at the house, she'd have to inspect their personal hygiene. I remember her telling Johnny Parker that he needed to rub harder when he washed behind his ears. She actually said, 'Young man, there's enough dirt behind those ears to grow potatoes.' Wouldn't you think she'd have been embarrassed? I was and I'm pretty sure Johnny was, too. She'd even smell somebody's breath to see if they had halitosis or, as she called it, 'hali.'

She'd also inspect my friends for head lice, fleas, bed bugs and who knows what else. It wasn't long before my friends wouldn't come into our house anymore, and I couldn't blame them. Just imagine if she pulled any of that nonsense with Molly Noonan on the bus ride to Fenway. That would have been sufficient reason to stop holding Molly's hand and pretending not to know her. That was a heroic gesture on my part because I liked holding her hand a lot. If it wasn't for my mother, I might have married Molly someday.

When Dr. Burrell started drilling, I noticed he had circles of sweat under his arms, so I tried not to smell his arm pits, the right one already was next to my face. The B.O. lady leaned on me harder, the noise got louder, there was a wicked sharp pain in my lower right jaw, then a smell from something burning and I could see smoke coming out of my mouth like I was smoking a Lucky. I did the only thing I could – I screamed bloody murder!

What happened was while the dentist was working on my tooth, the drill got stuck inside the cavity and Dr. Burrell was running it backward and forward trying to get it out of the hole like the way my father rocked our car back and forth when a rear wheel was stuck in the snow. I was in horrible pain and started screaming for help. There was nothing else I could do! Where were the cops when I needed them?

I tried to get out of the chair, but the assistant pressed harder. I remember shouting, 'Let me out,' over and over. I asked the dentist where the stuff was that was supposed to stop the pain, explaining what my father had told me. Dr. Burrell said he didn't use any of that 'new-fangled' stuff.

Then he resumed drilling away on my smoking tooth while the assistant crushed me against the black leather upholstery of the chair and sprayed cold water in my mouth. The cold water hurt as much as the drilling did! It was the worst pain I had ever felt, and it seemed like it went on for hours. All I could think about was that the drilling was more painful than having the stitches removed after the Carney Hospital surgery and that this was another case of my father lying to me about nothing bad happening when he knew better. I actually don't remember the tooth getting filled or even recall leaving the office. I must have been half unconscious from the pain. I promised myself I'd never go there again. A lot of good that did.

When I got home, nobody was there so I grabbed my fishing rod and dug up a few worms from under one of the flagstones in the walkway beside our garage. I figured that catching some fish at the pond would take my mind off my aching tooth, so I grabbed a pail from inside our shed to carry any fish I caught and headed for Sailors' Home Pond. The story in the neighborhood was that the pond was part of the original Sailors'

Home, a residence for disabled Navy veterans of the Civil War. A house, a barn, the pond, a cemetery, farmland and fields had occupied the knoll for fifty or sixty years after the war ended or until there were no veterans left, I figured.

The pond was at the bottom of a hill behind where the main building had been. It was surrounded by large trees, mostly weeping willows that created an eerie setting like someplace I'd seen in a Disney movie called Song of the South. At times when the water was warmer than the air, a fog would cover the pond and make it look spooky but there were still plenty of fish there. What looked even spookier was when fog would roll in from Quincy Bay and surround the headstones in the cemetery near the homemade baseball field. That looked like a scene from the movie, Abbott and Costello Meet Frankenstein, where the monster jumps out at them in a foggy graveyard. I think I dropped my popcorn when I saw that scene at the Wolly.

While I lived in the neighborhood, the City of Quincy stocked the pond with fish every spring so the fishing was always good and kids gathered there on the warmer days of summer for fishing and on the frozen days of winter, when the city put hockey nets on the ice so that older kids, like my brother Jimmy, could play hockey. Some kids used to say that living in our neighborhood was more fun than a barrel of monkeys. I don't know if that was true but rain or shine, heat or cold, the Beechwood Knoll was a fabulous neighborhood for kids!

Chapter Twenty-nine

The Ragman

Of all the visitors who came to our Wollaston Beach neighborhood, the most memorable was the ragman who every now and then appeared, as if out of nowhere, seated on the bench of a weather-worn wooden wagon, pulled by a sweaty, brown nag that looked like it was ready for the glue factory, as folks used to say about old horses.

The weary horse had a brown leather pouch of oats or hay strapped around its head as though stopping to feed the poor animal properly was too big an effort for the ragman. Nobody seemed to know anything about the mysterious driver of the wagon except Mike Dolan's mother who said that she heard that his name was Louie. It was pretty strange because Louie, the horse and wagon looked like a scene from the 19th century that I'd seen in a movie about the Civil War.

We'd know when Louie and his horse were coming by the sounds of the metal horseshoes striking the asphalt pavement in measured, slow-motion, clip-clop cadence as they came down Fenno Street from the direction of Hancock Street. The horseshoe cadence was regularly interrupted by the chanting of the old ragman as he slumped forward at the reins, forlornly chortling choruses of 'Rags, paper, junk. Rags, paper,

junk.' The only thing I could compare it to was the history lesson about Paul Revere riding a horse through the streets of Boston shouting, 'The British are coming.'

Louie was so unique that he was like a celebrity visitor from the pages of history who wasn't afraid of looking and acting different than everyone else. He wore a crumpled, soft felt hat with a turned-down brim that kept the sunlight off both his unshaven face and the back of his neck. His long-sleeve khaki work shirt and the matching stained pants he wore looked like rags he collected in his travels, ones that turned out to be just the right size for him. His face, at least the part I could see, didn't look as old as I expected, and I thought he looked like he might have been someone who once was important. He'd be hunched over the front of his wagon as though he was about to nod off. Of course, he never did nod off thanks to his incessant chant of 'Rags, paper, junk.'

Yet, all things considered, he looked like he could keep going for a few more years and my father praised the guy for getting up and going to work every day at his advanced age. He once said, 'You might be surprised some day to find out that the ragman has more money than the rest of us put together.'

Except for my mother, nobody really cared about what he was, least of all me. His nationality, race or religion just didn't matter. It was hard for me to believe that anyone would still be riding around in a horse-drawn wagon because cars, trucks and buses had monopolized the streets of Quincy for longer than I'd been alive. Even though Hancock Street still had rails from the streetcars that used to be used for public transportation, streetcars and horse-drawn wagons were a thing of the past.

The neighborhood kids used to guess their ages, Louie and the horse. I once heard someone ask Louie about their ages, but he didn't interrupt his diligent surveillance of the road ahead to give an answer. My guess was that he was close to 80 because the wagon looked to be from the year one. The wheels holding up the wobbly wooden wagon were so rickety that it looked like one of them might fall off at any second and roll into the pond, the marsh or the bay before toppling Louie and the horse over.

My mother saved our newspapers, grocery bags and worn-out clothing for the ragman because she figured the old guy was probably broke and whatever she gave him might help to keep him and his horse from starving for another day. It was one of her 'good deeds,' as she put it, an example of her charitable work, like the quarter she dropped into the straw collection basket at St. Ann's, or the dime she'd drop in one of the metal stands that held the holy candles. Most times the ragman offered my mother a few pennies for her paper and rags, but she took pride in thinking that he needed the pennies more than she did. I was impressed by her generosity. You'd have thought she was a nun, like one of the Little Sisters of the Poor.

And here's why I've drawn out this story about the ragman. It's because my mother used to love to look at new houses when my father was around. She frequently asked my father to take her for a ride to see some of the new houses in Quincy or Milton.

I was with them on the day my father took her to see a new house on Quincy's Furnace Brook Parkway, a winding picturesque road and one of my mother's favorite places. The house was a single story, red brick ranch-style with a two-car garage, new lawn, a grove of white birch trees and a babbling brook. My mother asked my father to go slower so she could get a better look, and to turn around and pass the house going in the other direction where it would be closer to her side of the car.

She raved about how beautiful the house was. She said that someday she'd love to live in a house like that. And she asked my father how much the house was worth, since he knew a lot about construction costs. Whatever the number he quoted, she was overwhelmed by it and guessed that the owner must have been the president of a Boston bank, or a major business like the Fore River Shipyard.

My father said, 'If I told you who lives there, you'd drop dead from shock.'

That started her curiosity rising like a hot-air balloon. She begged him to tell her who the owner was, and he teased her for a while before giving her the answer. Finally, he caved in and shared the information with her, something for which she was totally unprepared.

According to my father, the owner was an eccentric guy who rode around Quincy in a horse-drawn wagon collecting rags. His name was Louie Grossman, and my father described him as being 'filthy rich.' Supposedly, he had founded a chain of lumber yards and hardware stores that carried his last name. And everyone around Quincy knew about Grossman's Lumber Yard near Quincy Center. The orange-and-white delivery trucks had 'Here Comes Grossman's' painted on the front, and 'There goes Grossman's' on the back.

My father told her that the ragman was a millionaire who had made a fortune from his business which, believe it or not, included collecting rags, paper and junk.

I'd never seen my mother's face turn that red. Her generosity turned into envy, as though the ragman had been pretending to be poor so he could build a better house than hers. You would have thought the guy had lied to her and stolen her money. Maybe she felt he had. There was a popular radio show at the time, which later became a TV show, called The Life of Riley in which the leading character, Chester A. Riley, would often say in a pathetic voice, 'What a revoltin' development this is.'

That seemed to summarize my mother's reaction to my father's news about the beautiful house on Furnace Brook Parkway. She went into a tirade meant to teach me some lessons about finance.

She told me to learn from what I had just seen. She said, 'Charity begins at home, so don't be throwing money away like I did on the ragman. That guy can buy and sell the rest of us.' That was followed by, 'Don't ever forget that money will always be your best friend, so put enough money away for a rainy day because you never know when you're going to need it.'

Even after five minutes or more, my mother looked like she might drop dead from shock over the news about the ragman's house. I never found out if my father's ragman story was actually true, but it didn't matter. My father had told me many times to never judge a book by its cover, and the ragman was a perfect example of why. I'd always thought that my father had wisdom, but it wasn't until that day that the realization struck me that he also had a sense of humor. There were times when my mother showed a sense of humor too, but never when it came to the topic of money.

Chapter Thirty

He might kill him!

My parents wanted things to be done according to their rules, even if their rules didn't make any sense to other people. And it didn't do any good to complain. My father's repeated threat was: 'If you don't shut up, I'll give you something to really complain about,' and we all knew he could. I can't count how many times I heard him say it. Although I wasn't sure what he might actually do, it didn't sound like anything I wanted to find out about. But to my regret, there came a day when I did.

I was in our basement in Wollaston during 4th

grade, when I saw my father hitting my brother in the head so hard that I thought to myself, he might kill him! I figured I might never survive a beating like that one because my father had the biggest hands and arms I'd ever seen. Plus, I figured he must have had a vicious, mean streak to physically abuse someone who'd gone through the amount of facial surgery that Jimmy had, not to mention that Jimmy was his son. Even though I was just a kid, I didn't think that I'd ever be able to beat up someone I loved! How could my father do it to Jimmy? And if he did it to Jimmy, what would stop him from doing the same to me?

I ran up two flights of stairs to the bedrooms and made my way through the walk-in closet in my sisters' room, where there was a short set of stairs to the attic. I closed the closet door, and I sat alone in the dimly lit humidity, crying about what my father had done to Jimmy. Was I the only one who cared about Jimmy? And why did I care since Jimmy never seemed to care about me?

After that incident, Jimmy didn't live with us anymore and, since I didn't want to get evicted from the house, I tried to behave better. Dorothy had moved out by then and I heard only that she went to Hollywood to try to become a movie star. With Dorothy and Jimmy gone, things weren't much fun because I was left with Barbara who, by then, was a double grouch. I pretty much avoided her, and she did the same to me. She was always whining about me touching her stuff, like she had anything worth touching. Well, actually she did have one thing – the forty-five RPM record player with an automatic record changer. She also had a handful of records that I liked to watch being automatically dropped onto the turntable. She always seemed to know when I'd been monkeying around with it, too. She said she could recognize my greasy little fingerprints and she'd start screaming and slam her bedroom door! When Barbara had a temper tantrum, you had to move fast to escape the rage rampage.

Probably what saved Jimmy from getting seriously hurt from the basement beating was that he was so strong and athletic. Compared to him, I looked like a scarecrow. In fact, I didn't look like Jimmy at all. For that matter, I didn't look like Barbara or Dorothy either. Jimmy had an athletic build that made him look like a boxer or a wrestler. I was skinny as a twig. When Jimmy was shirtless, my mother used to call him 'Brave Hercules' because he was so muscular. Me? You'd never catch me shirtless because when I turned sideways, I'd practically disappear.

Jimmy looked to me like Charles Atlas, the guy pictured on the back cover of comic books, dressed in a leopard skin Speedo bathing suit, claiming to be the world's strongest man. The comic book headline read, 'Hey Skinny, why be a ninety-eight-pound weakling when you can have muscles like mine?' It was an advertisement for a mail order weightlifting and exercise program, but Jimmy already looked like Charles Atlas as far as I was concerned.

I not only looked like the ninety-eight-pound weakling in the ad, but I weighed only half that much. My arms looked like toothpicks and my legs resembled wooden drumsticks. Jimmy could do about 50 pushups with each arm; I couldn't do one pushup with both arms without my elbows killing me! Yes sir, if my father had ever hit me in the head, as hard as I saw him hitting Jimmy, I could have been as dead as a doornail or like one of the boulders in the Wollaston Beach sea wall.

Who ever thought that my brother would wind up renting a furnished room in a crummy section of Boston after he'd been banished from our house because he stole a $100 savings bond from my father's office and denied doing it. All I remember about the incident was that Jimmy owed the money to a bookie because he had been betting on horse races and losing. What I've never forgotten was how my father beat the snot out of Jimmy when he confronted him about the lie and then threw him out of the house, telling him not to ever come back. Barbara and I both cried hard about that turn of events, as we looked out a bedroom window, watching Jimmy walking away in a pouring rainstorm.

A month or so later, my father dragged me along to visit Jimmy at the rooming house where he was living in Boston. I couldn't believe how small it was – one room with a closet. The building had a public toilet down the hall that Jimmy and the other renters shared. When my father and I left there, I was broken-hearted because my brother was living in such a dump when we had plenty of room at our house. My father called Jimmy's place a 'flop house' and said the neighborhood was one of the worst slums in Boston. I wondered, 'So, why are you making him live there?'

I cried after my father and I left and I was mad because I couldn't do anything to help Jimmy. My father said he was teaching Jimmy a lesson. I wanted to scream at him, grab him by his throat and punch him in the head, but I couldn't because I was terrified of him. The man was a tyrant and a bully, and I didn't want to suffer the same punishment as Jimmy had received.

Visiting Jimmy reminded me of that day when we lived near Chicago and my father put Jimmy on a train by himself to get mouth and nose surgery a thousand miles away. I cried then, too, because there was some sort of a disconnect between the two of them – James A. Murphy, Sr. and James A. Murphy, Jr. It was just wrong, that's all there was to it, and it never got any better. We had a spare bedroom in the house in Wollaston and I'd have loved it if Jimmy came back to live with us. Heck, he could have slept in my new bed, and I'd have gone back to sleeping in one of the bunk beds. But my father wouldn't budge – Jimmy was on his own and that's all there was to it. It wasn't even a topic for conversation with either of my parents.

That was the year when the second story and roof of the Wollaston Yacht Club burned. Although it was unfortunate for the membership, it was another example of the interesting things that happened in and around the Wollaston Beach Area. It seemed that everyone I knew went there on the Thursday afternoon following the fire and for a week or two after to watch the demolition and repairs.

Soon enough, I was thrilled when my mother told

me that my father was going to take me and her to the Ringling Brothers Circus at Boston Garden. I knew nothing about Boston Garden except that Boston's pro basketball team, the Celtics, and its pro hockey team, the Bruins, played games there. I remember that we had to walk around in circles as we went up the ramp to our seats, which were pretty high up. It was called a three-ring circus and the acts were really exciting – clowns, trained animals, acrobats, trapeze artists, tightrope walkers, jugglers, magicians, cyclists and a compact car with twenty clowns.

I was definitely captivated. But the sideshow was way too creepy for me. My mother called it the 'freak' show and I felt badly for the people involved. There was a fat lady, a bearded lady, a woman with tattoos, men with tattoos on practically every body part, giant people, little people and all kinds of other people. My mother said there might be Siamese twins with two heads, but I had seen enough. I did see a black snake with two heads, but that part of the circus was so depressing that I had no interest in going again.

Chapter Thirty-one

Up on the roof

It wasn't much longer before Christmas rolled around; 4th grade was the first time my father included me in setting up a tree. He had an amazing scheme for choosing, shaping and decorating a tree that took about three days. He began by visiting about a dozen tree vendors located between the Neponset River Bridge in North Quincy and the Fore River Bridge in South Quincy until he found the exact tree he wanted. It was usually about two or three feet taller than the space where he intended to erect it. After negotiating the price, he tied it onto the roof of his Buick and brought it home.

In our garage, he cut enough of the trunk and branches off the bottom so that the remaining trunk would fit inside the ring of the red and green metal stand. From the top he removed enough branches and trunk so that the tree would fit just below the living room ceiling beneath the corner of the roof toward the front of the house. From the inside of the house, it looked like the top of the tree must have gone through the ceiling and come out up on the roof.

The process involved using a measuring tape, a spirit level, a hand saw, an electric drill, a roll of twine, several screw hooks and a half-dozen electrical, extension cords. I was reminded of the mad scientist I had seen in another Frankenstein movie. My father had me hold the tree upright while he used the spirit level to get it straight or 'plumb' as he called it. Then he installed the screw hooks into the wooden, window trim on two walls and tied pieces of twine from the trunk to the hooks to keep the tree upright in the corner he had chosen.

That was the easy part. Next came wrapping the 40

strings of light sockets around the boughs, including about 600 colored bulbs and connecting the cords together from the wall outlet near the floor, then from one to another from bottom to top. He'd determine where there were larger gaps between branches, cut some of the boughs he'd removed earlier, drill holes into the trunk and insert the branches into the holes, filling the gaps.

When he was done with that, everybody who was at home would start hanging the ornaments, while debating where each of them should be located. My mother cooked popcorn kernels that turned into little white flowers that Barbara could make into garlands by running a needle and thread through all of them. The final touches were silver icicles that would adorn the tips of the branches, making our tree look like a greeting card picture of a tree in a snowy forest. My mother would then spread a white, double bed sheet on the floor so everyone could put presents underneath the auspicious tree. The biggest hazard was always the dog's tail, when it wagged, striking the tree ornaments. So, the dog would be banned from the living room until after Christmas.

What was extra special about that Christmas was my father bought me a set of Lionel electric trains, which he set-up on the living room floor after I went to bed on Christmas Eve. The engine had a working headlight, a smokestack that puffed out smoke and a whistle that sounded like the real deal. What an excellent surprise it was on Christmas morning except I hated going to the eleven-thirty Mass at St. Ann's instead of staying home to play with the train set.

Although I'd seen a huge Christmas tree at the Jordan Marsh department store in Boston, I still thought my father's tree looked excellent. I had never known anyone who was as finicky about decorating a Christmas tree but that was how he was. My mother explained that his family never had a Christmas tree when he was a kid, so he was trying to make sure that his children appreciated the joy of Christmas. Although gruff on the surface, my father had a soft spot inside of him when it came to Christmas.

Meantime, the rest of us had to endure his complaining during the process – you know, those profanities that parents aren't supposed to say out loud when kids are around. You'd hear him huffing and puffing and cursing now and then, muttering words that sounded, from a distance, like, 'You dirty ratzenfratzen.' There'd be a pile of cigarette ashes and butts in his gigantic, green glass ash tray. And, when all was said and done, we'd know when it was safe to enter the living room by the smell of cigar smoke from one of his El Producto Corona cigars. That behavior for my father was like the winning driver at the Indy 500 taking a victory lap or like the Catholic College of Cardinals indicating that a new pope had been elected by sending a smoke signal to the world.

Summer came, the year following 4th grade. My father told me he was pleased with my behavior and my schoolwork. He had sent me several post cards from cities where he went on business trips during the school year, places like New York, Chicago and Montreal.

Once he wrote me a letter on hotel stationary from Hartford saying if I kept up the good work, he would buy me that English racing bike. That was fabulous news!

After school ended, I found out that my cousin Arch, who owned a warehouse near Roxbury Crossing, had a contract with the Boston Police Department that permitted the police to store stolen property there until a trial had determined what was to happen to the stolen goods. In some cases, property would be raffled off to the public. By some tricky shenanigans, Arch had gotten someone in the police department to agree to let my father make the only bid for a red Rolfe racing bike. Arch delivered the bike to our house on the Saturday afternoon after the raffle. That was a most exciting event indeed!

One of the first trips I made on the new bike was to Squantum Naval Air Station at the Dorchester end of Wollaston Beach. My friends and I were anxious to see the acrobatic group of Navy jet fighter pilots named the Blue Angels. It would be my first time to see jet fighters. The planes that were regularly being used for training at Squantum were WWII propellor models and were very slow compared to the newer style F-9 Panther jets being used beginning in 1948.

The Panther jets were much faster and made a shrill whistling noise as they flew past us. The planes were painted in shiny blue and gold colors with the words, 'Blue Angels' on the sides. They flew through the air, climbing at breakneck speeds, then swooped down toward the ground. Each time the six-plane formation came closer to the field where the crowd was gathered and what a crowd it was! The announcer at the aerial show said the Panther jets could fly 200 miles per hour faster than most propellor fighter planes and could climb nearly twice as fast. That was exciting stuff for kids to watch, another benefit of living in our neighborhood. On the way back to the Beechwood Knoll, we pretended our bikes were F-9s and that we were pilots doing aerial stunts when all I was really doing were wheelies on my rear tire.

At the time we watched the Blue Angels, how could I have known that in less than two years, Ted Williams would begin flying combat missions over North Korea, 39 of them, for the U.S. Marine Corps, while doing a second tour of active duty. How could I have known that a future astronaut and future U.S. Senator – John Glenn – would select Williams as the best wingman in the Korean war. And why wouldn't he since Ted was the recipient of fifteen medals and awards for valor. Three of his flights were struck by enemy ground fire, one ending in a crash landing. Ted received the Department of Defense Air Medal three times with two gold stars, the Navy Commendation Medal for outstanding heroism against the enemy, three campaign medals with two bronze stars, the U.S. Presidential medal of Freedom and a chest full of other awards. Captain Theodore Samuel Williams was a top-notch combat pilot as well as one of the best baseball players in the history of Major League Baseball in spite of missing five seasons due to his military service.

Life went on, and I had no choice but to move right

along with it. We were one of the last families in the neighborhood to get a television set because my father was waiting for a big screen. Laugh if you want, but a sixteen-inch screen was the biggest anyone sold in December of 1949, and when RCA introduced it, my father bought one. You could be sure, if he bought the thing, it was made in America.

He paid the preposterous price of $600 for a mahogany sixteen-inch, table-model TV with a four-legged matching stand. He said he bought it from the appliances department of the Jordan Marsh department store in Boston. My mother thought my father was out of his mind because, at that time, $600 was the cost of a year of college tuition and half the price of a new Chevy, Plymouth or Ford sedan.

Our TV had knobs for selecting channels, volume, brightness and contrast. It was state of the art technology for 1949 and it took two people to lift the darned thing because it was made out of wood, metal and glass – nothing was solid-state or digital in those days and not much was made from plastics yet. Other than getting my first bike, if I had to name the most memorable day in my life up until that point, it would be the snowy afternoon when I had forgotten to wear galoshes to school and had to trudge through about a foot of the white stuff while coming home. Although my feet were soaked and nearly frozen, I saw that big-screen TV through our living room window as I walked up to the front door. The set was in the right rear corner of our living room, and I was awestruck when I got inside the house and saw it.

When my father asked me to help him move the TV set to another location, we could barely budge it. The TV set felt like our living room sofa. According to my father, because we had to wait for vacuum tubes inside the set to warm up, it took about three minutes before we could see a clear picture of anything. Nevertheless, having a TV was like graduating from prehistoric times into the space age, even though all the programs were telecast in black and white.

I also remember that day because a kid in my 4th grade class named Bobby Craig had convinced me to go with him after school to the house of a girl in our class named Jeanette Berard who lived behind the Supreme Market on Hancock Street, practically in North Quincy. Jeanette was someone he wanted to invite to a movie. He was afraid to ask her without moral support, so I promised to go with him even though I had absolutely no experience with dating. Looking back, I can't tell you why I agreed because I knew absolutely nothing about dealing with girls.

At home, I got so excited about the big-screen TV and about the war movie that my father was watching about U.S. Marines landing on a beach in a place called Tripoli that I forgot all about my frozen feet. The TV excitement must have made my heart pump faster because I never had to have any toes amputated in spite of the long walk through the freezing snow.

Yet even though we got the TV, I didn't get to see a professional baseball game because, as I said earlier, my mother heard at the beauty parlor that watching TV could ruin a kid's eyesight. So, I had to listen to

Red Sox games played inside my plastic, RCA table-model radio, which I'd sometimes put beside me on my mattress and pull the covers over my head so my mother wouldn't know I was listening to a night game in the dark. I had an attraction to baseball that I couldn't explain and listening to a game while falling asleep was the best way of drifting off to dreamland.

Chapter Thirty-two

Patriotism

There was an outstanding event that happened once in the Beechwood Knoll, and I can't for the life of me remember which year it was or what grade I was about to enter at the time. The event was Quincy's Fourth of July parade, which was an annual favorite, and one year it took place in our neighborhood. I asked my sister Barbara if she remembered what year that was, thinking she might since she was a baton twirler at Quincy High School around that time. For all I knew, she might have been in the parade but no such luck – Barbara had no recollection of it. We concluded that it probably took place after she graduated from high school, married and left home for Salzburg, Austria by way of Paris, Brussels and Frankfort to join her husband, George Butler, who had enlisted in the Army. If I've figured correctly, I would have been attending Central Junior High School by then, which was probably 1952.

Anyway, this was no short parade; this was part of Quincy's celebration of patriotism. Around noontime, on a gorgeous, sunny day, the parade formed at the bus stop diagonally across from our house and extended backward up Fenno toward Hancock Street. The parade was about a half mile long and starting at the bus stop, it moved forward, down Fenno Street toward the baseball field, made a left turn onto Andrews Road, came up to our corner, then turned right onto Havilend Street heading toward the beach.

At the front was a Quincy Police motorcycle with blinking red lights under the handlebars. Our Fenno Street neighbor, Officer Bill Spencer, was driving it wearing his cap, shirt, riding pants, black boots, gun belt, holster and pistol. He was Julie Kirkland's uncle; Julie was my classmate who asked me if we could kiss once. Officer Bill was the nicest cop I'd ever met and let's not forget that I'd met more than a few cops in my life of crime. Imagine me liking a cop after all the stuff I'd been through!

Next was a black convertible carrying state representative Joe Brett and his wife, two more of our Fenno Street neighbors. Then came a marching band that was a drum and bugle corps from a Catholic Church. I'd seen the marching bands from Quincy and North Quincy High Schools at Thanksgiving Day football games at Veteran's Memorial Stadium, but those bands were much larger. The band members in our parade wore green uniforms with silver trim and low, green hats with long, bushy white feathers. The rat-tatty-tat-tat drum cadences were mixed with blaring shrieks from the horns, and it was so thrilling I wanted to jump off our front steps and join in marching. The uniforms made the band members look like Robin Hood and his band of merry men that I'd seen in a copy of a painting at the Wollaston branch of the Quincy Public Library. Their music was fabulously loud, and I still remember how exhilarating it was.

Then came a Quincy fire truck, a hook and ladder no less. There were plenty of red, flashing lights and a siren that practically punctured my eardrums. It was followed by a horse-drawn wagon carrying bales of hay and a group of seated children waving miniature American flags. Behind the wagon was a golden Palomino horse with a white mane and tail that looked like Trigger, the horse Roy Rogers rode in his movies. Only this rider was a man named Cowboy Bob from radio station WJDA in Quincy who had a Saturday morning program for kids.

My Cub Scouts den had gone to his program once, taken there by Jackie Thurston's mother, our den leader. In the parade, Bob's wife was riding a horse that my father called a chestnut mare. I still remember the day I met Mr. and Mrs. Cowboy Bob because I had been awarded my Cub Scouts' lion badge the night before and my mother had sewed it, together with some arrow awards for my wolf and bear badges, to my dark blue uniform shirt. At the WJDA studio we had a picture taken in our uniforms the next day with Bob and his wife, a great day made better the following week when the picture appeared in the Quincy Patriot

Ledger. I also remember that I almost missed the visit to the studio because my father forgot to wake me up on time and I had to rush like mad to get dressed.

Although there were a bunch of other parade attractions, including some war hero types who were members of the American Legion, those are the things I remember best plus Officer Bill Spencer waving to me as he passed our corner. He gave a short blast on his siren and called out my name which made my father question how I knew another motorcycle cop, other than the one who met us at school after I stuck-up the 6th grade girl. I don't remember my answer, but it must have been a good one because I didn't get blamed for doing anything wrong.

But it wasn't a great day just because of the parade, it was also a great afternoon and night because our neighbors always had a block party on the Fourth and that year was no different. Whoever heard of living in a quiet, residential neighborhood where a holiday parade went past your front door? Whoever heard of having a block party in the street where you lived on the same day? If that wasn't enough excitement for one day, there were still fireworks about to happen after dark. As I said, there was a lot of patriotism following WWII. As I also said, there was plenty of interesting activities at and near the Beechwood Knoll.

For the block party, part of Havilend Street was blocked off with red, wooden sawhorses and decorated with various colors of Japanese lanterns strung between the sticky, skinny oak trees next to the sidewalks. There was music playing through loudspeakers and people were dancing in the street and enjoying food and drinks. It was funny to watch the older women doing fancy, high-stepping dances in public and they seemed to be having a great time.

My mother wanted to go to the party, but my father refused and that was all there was to that discussion. I thought it was great because everything was free, and I drank enough Cokes to have the biggest burp ever. After dark, the boulevard would be crammed with cars waiting for the fireworks show to begin at Merrymount Beach. That was within walking distance, but we took our bikes to get there quicker. That's the way life was when you were a kid back then – hurry up and wait... for the next thing to do. The show lasted about a half hour, and I was worn out from oohing and aahing and had a crick in my next from looking straight up at the sky when the last skyrocket explosions occurred. The last ones were red, white and blue, of course.

Looking back at life in our neighborhood, I realize how compartmentalized it was. The Beechwood Knoll was somewhat different than any other neighborhood I knew about. To some extent, we had a different perspective on life than if we had lived in Houghs Neck or Quincy Point or West Quincy or Squantum not to mention other cities or states. That's just the way it was after WWII, and we accepted it.

It was a place where prejudice and segregation were commonplace, even as to what vendors people dealt with. For instance, our milk was delivered by a tan, Hood Milk Company van while the Dolans had their milk delivered by a white van from White Brothers. To

Mike Dolan that was a big deal and he'd argue about how much better his milk was than mine. It was the same with newspaper deliveries, whether it was The Boston Globe or The Boston Herald Traveler. Then came the issue of the brand of car your family had – General Motors, Ford or Chrysler. We argued about everything.

There were more serious issues too, like whether your family was Catholic or Protestant, Irish or Italian, Democrat or Republican. I think everyone in the knoll was Caucasian. although I don't know why, except that was also true of my school. The only other folks I'd see were the Chinese people at the Star of the Sea restaurant and Johnny Parker who lived two blocks away. It was a time when what you were seemed to be more important than who you were. The only people my mother called by their names were the Irish. That would have been the Dolans, the Degans, the O'Briens, the Rileys, the Ahearns, the O'Donnells, the Egans, etc.

To her, people she couldn't categorize as easily were known by their religion, nationality or occupation. And all Italians were known to her by the name Botchagaloopie. That was because my sister Dorothy was asked out on a date by a boy named Fred Bottolotti. My mother couldn't wrap her mind around how that was pronounced so she gave him the monicker, Joe Botchagaloopie, which became her catch-all name for all Italians.

Any other people with complicated names would arouse the question, 'Do you spell that with a wee or a wubayou?' That was my mother, all right. Unless a person was Irish-Catholic, they were second-rate citizens according to her. Unless Irish or Italian, my mother had to know everybody's background so that she could describe them in a way that circumvented her prejudices like 'the bus driver's wife,' 'the Polish woman with the tattoo,' and 'the Jewish woman with the white fence.'

Chapter Thirty-three

Run for your life

I'm pretty sure that the Fourth of July parade occurred during the same summer that my mother had pestered my father endlessly about teaching her how to drive until he finally caved in... well, sort of that is. Actually, he still refused to teach her and refused to let her drive his black Buick but, as a compromise, he offered to pay for her to take driving lessons from a woman whose husband was in my father's AA group. I was shocked when he paid twenty-five dollars for her lessons, five of them.

The woman had her own car, which was equipped with dual brake pedals so she could operate what she called a driving school. Her car was equipped with a standard shift transmission because people had to know how to drive with standard shift to pass the test at that time. That was my father's excuse for not letting my mother practice on his car – driving tests were offered with standard shift only and the Buick had automatic. A perfect alibi for him!

In our neighborhood, only a handful of women had driver's licenses. My father was entirely opposed to the whole idea. He used to warn people that whenever they saw a woman driver headed their way to immediately 'run for your life' because women drivers were a hazard to pedestrians, pets and property. He wasn't the only man in the neighborhood who was opposed to women drivers, either. There were probably more women drivers' jokes than any other kind. My father once told me, 'There ought to be a law against women drivers, and since there isn't, I'd be the first guy to vote for one.' I believed him and believed he was deadly serious about it.

I had thought that my father didn't have any prejudices until then, but he had enough dislike for women drivers to make up for all the prejudices he didn't have. He once said he wouldn't let Dorothy or Barbara drive his car under any circumstances, although I had been with him once when he let Jimmy try driving. He hollered so loudly that Jimmy became a nervous wreck and nearly drove us over a cliff. Jimmy was never given another chance, as far as I know.

What further complicated my father's reluctance to let my mother drive was that she had no mechanical aptitude and was terrified of electrical and gas appliances. She would prefer to keep the vacuum set so that it started running at her preferred setting when she plugged it in. The radio was left set at one station, the furnace at one temperature and the oven at another.

When something needed to be adjusted, she would ask somebody else to do it, even changing a light bulb. It certainly made me wonder how she would ever get the hang of driving a car.

In those days, the custom was for the man to drive the family car and most people accepted it. Whether husbands drove to work or took a bus, the wives would usually stay at home during the day, meaning the car would stay in the garage. Very few mothers had jobs and the ones with infants were expected to be 'stay-at-home moms.' That was why daily deliveries of goods and services were commonplace.

If my mother needed to go somewhere, she'd take the local bus and transfer to another bus or to the subway to get there. On rare occasions, she'd take a cab, but the cost was usually prohibitive. She'd rather wait until Saturday when my father would be home. That was an unpleasant task for him but better than the option of letting her get a driver's license and, God forbid, drive his four-thousand-pound, four-thousand-dollar Buick.

That issue became an almost nightly dispute, and my mother became more insulted and angrier. Finally, my father agreed to pay the driving instructor and, if by some unlikely miracle, the Commonwealth of Massachusetts, Registry of Motor Vehicles gave my mother a license, he'd talk about her using the Buick if he thought she could handle it. He sounded supremely confident that there was no chance of that ever happening. Afterward, I heard my father say to his friend, Joe Doherty, that there was absolutely no chance of her ever getting a license.

After her first lesson, I'd have bet my life she wasn't going to get a license because she refused to wear her eyeglasses. When I asked her why, she said she didn't want any of our neighbors to know that she wore glasses and that she didn't want the instructor to know that she had poor eyesight. After that, I would never have gotten into any car, of my own free will, that she was driving. Yikes! It seemed comparable to riding in a car driven by Helen Keller, the blind woman who was a special needs activist.

After five lessons, the driving test was scheduled to take place at North Quincy High School. My mother's instructor suggested to my father that my mother needed more practice, and he should be willing to let her try driving the Buick around the neighborhood, since she'd need to know how to drive it if she got a license. When my father agreed, I knew one thing – I wasn't going to get into any car she was driving if I could possibly avoid it. But my father ordered me to get into the Buick's back seat the next day and said if he was going to be in an accident, I was going to be in one, too. What the heck did that mean? Then I realized that he might have been right about an accident since the Buick had only one set of pedals.

Although she was able to reach the emergency brake, from the moment my mother couldn't find the ignition switch, couldn't figure how to shift into the drive position and got her right shoe caught under the brake pedal, the experiment was a disaster. My father went ballistic, calling her every humiliating name I'd

ever heard. He kept shouting at her at the top of his voice until he reached over and put the shift lever into drive himself. He was so furious that I thought he was going to strangle her. By that time, I already had my right hand on the rear door handle, ready to jump out if necessary.

The car was parked on the street in front of our house, facing downhill. As Murphy's Law would predict, the car began to roll forward, which terrified my mother, causing her to scream. She yanked on the driver's door handle, pushed the door open and stepped out of the car onto the street as the black Buick rolled past her without a driver. When I glanced at her, she was straightening her dress, as though completely oblivious to the hazard she had created.

My father grabbed the wheel from the passenger's seat with his left hand and yanked it to the right, causing the car to roll up over the curb stone and come to a stop partly on the sidewalk and partly on our front lawn. Once he put the shift lever into park, he was so infuriated that I thought his head was about to explode, releasing a burst of magma and boulders that would blow a hole through the roof of the Buick. The car had only traveled about ten yards, but I was convinced that my mother's driving career was as over as WWII was over.

So, I prayed that my father wouldn't have a stroke, that my mother wouldn't suffer from lifelong depression and that I would be able to stop shaking from fright from the failed. experiment. Truthfully, I was ecstatic that she wouldn't be driving because she might have killed someone including herself, me and most of our neighbors. I never heard my parents discussing the driving subject again, which was a very good result.

Soon afterward, Mike Dolan's father died, and Mrs. Dolan decided to get a job. But she didn't have a driver's license and would need a car to commute to her job. I don't remember who gave her driving lessons but somehow, she managed to get a license. I was flabbergasted! The following Sunday she invited my mother and me to join her and Mike for a fall foliage drive to New Hampshire in the Studebaker she bought. My mother insisted that I go because she didn't trust Mrs. Dolan's ability to drive. Well, for Pete's sake, neither did I, but I didn't have a license either. When she picked us up, Mike wasn't with her. Apparently, he knew better.

So, off we went without Mike. About an hour later, Mrs. Dolan decided to pass another car where there wasn't any passing lane. As I shouted to her that we couldn't pass, an oncoming car was heading smack dab toward us. At the last second, Mrs. Dolan yanked the steering wheel of the Studebaker to the right, which resulted in her car slamming into the car beside us. The other driver began blowing his horn and shaking his fist at us. Mrs. Dolan accelerated, drove through a red light and acted like the driver of a getaway car leaving the scene of a bank robbery! She was able to ditch the other driver and get us home safely, although I kept my eyes closed most of the way. That was the one and only time I rode with her, and it convinced me that my father might have been right about women drivers, at least some of them.

The next time I trusted a woman driver was when my sister Barbara's best friend, Jean, got a red Mercury convertible as a high school graduation gift. My mother occasionally made Barbara take me with her if she wanted to go somewhere with Jean. The first place that I remember going to was a car upholstery shop at the Neponset River Bridge, where Jean had leopard skin seat covers installed. That was pretty cool – a red convertible with leopard skin seats.

I never turned-down a chance to ride in Jean's Merc, woman driver or not! Anyway, I took a chance that Jean was a more trustworthy driver because she was younger. My mother was nearly fifty at the time she tried learning, which made her an old woman in my eyes.

Chapter Thirty-four

Gone forever

Nothing very dramatic happened from the time I began attending Central Junior High School, starting in the fall of 1951, until the conclusion of my sophomore year of high school. Then it happened – Jimmy was killed in an automobile accident! There was no mistake about it, Jimmy was dead! No matter how firmly I refused to believe it, my brother, Jimmy, was gone forever.

It was May 19, 1955, a Thursday night. I was at home studying for the next day's final exam in 10th grade geometry at Thayer Academy in Braintree. The front doorbell rang about eight PM and was answered by my mother, who was confronted by two Quincy Police officers. They asked to speak to my father. When he came to the door, I heard one of the cops tell him that Jimmy and another fellow were dead. Just like that – no warning, no sympathy, no nothing! The cop looked him in the eye and said that my brother was dead, killed in an automobile accident in Pelham, New Hampshire. My first thought was that I'd never get to be with him again - NEVER!

The story was that their rental car had been speeding on a country road and, whoever was driving lost control of the car. When the car flipped over, both occupants were ejected and later died from their injuries. Because the scene had been so torn apart by the force of the accident, none of the emergency people could determine who had been driving.

At that moment I felt like I had died in the accident. Poor Jimmy Wah-Wah was gone forever, and I never got to really know him even though I was fifteen-years-old at the time and had lived with Jimmy for most of my life. I'd always had a secret wish that someday after I moved out of the house, I would get to know him, and we'd become pals like we should have been from the beginning. Now that dream was also dead.

My parents didn't want to talk much about Jimmy's death after the cops left, and the three of us sat in our living room looking straight ahead. My parents were on opposite ends of the room, not expressing any visible emotion. They didn't hug or kiss or cry or anything, except sit and stare. Inwardly I was sobbing like a baby and felt ashamed because my father had no patience for people who cried. It was a sign of weakness to him. I figured the reason that my mother wasn't crying was because she knew he'd order her to shut up if she did.

Finally, my mother broke the silence by asking him what he was going to do about the situation and, to my dismay, the two of them had an unemotional discussion about it, like they were planning where they were going to shop for groceries on Saturday. I couldn't take it any longer and trudged up the stairs to my bedroom, fell face down onto my pillow and wept profusely, like I'd never done before. It was like I lost control of all the tears I'd been storing for fifteen years. I don't remember anything else until morning arrived.

When my mother awakened me, she was already in action mode, planning to go to New Hampshire with my father to view the scene of the accident and the wrecked car. That's what we did, and it was absolutely gruesome. My father had telephoned the police department there and spoken to the local sheriff, who met us at the scene. My father acted like he was a criminal investigator, asking a bunch of questions, including where Jimmy had landed on the road and where the car wound up.

When I saw the blood on the sandy asphalt from Jimmy's head injuries, I wanted to vomit but couldn't. I was shaking from crying so hard while trying to pretend I wasn't bothered by it at all. When my father wanted to see the rental car, my mother didn't, but she was overruled. We followed the sheriff to a brown barn. Outside, there was a yellow car, a 1955 Plymouth that had been rented from Avis. The hood was bent straight upward from the force of the impact, and it was hard to recognize because it seemed to have been smashed on every side, including the roof. It looked like the car had rolled over when it went off the road and smashed into a tree, a boulder or something just as hard.

The sheriff was an older man with scruffy gray hair and a Texas Ranger style cowboy hat who told my father that the car had been traveling close to 100 miles per hour and that Jimmy and a guy named George Lane had been racing up and down the road showing off to two girls who were walking along near the accident site. Reportedly, they were blowing the horn and waving out the windows. I thought the sheriff was a rat for making the story into a melodrama. Why would he tell us all those grotesque details? I figured he wanted to seem like some big shot by bashing my brother after he was dead. Poor Jimmy Wah-Wah couldn't catch a break in life or in death. It always seemed that fate was against him no matter what he did.

I couldn't help thinking about what a beautiful, warm sunlit day it was where we were standing – blue sky with billowy white clouds over a serene setting of giant green pine trees. I also couldn't help thinking about how poor Jimmy was lying in a morgue somewhere, no longer able to see anything or feel anything or even know that I had always loved him, because I never told him. Love wasn't something we discussed in our family.

To make it even worse, the sheriff said Jimmy's body was so badly mutilated that an undertaker probably wouldn't be able to leave the casket open. The guy was a total jerk, even if he was a sheriff – some small-town moron dressed up like a cowboy. A know-it-all little twirp probably giving the performance of his life. It had to be more exciting to him than chasing a lost cow or two, or a chicken thief. And the guy didn't care that he was doing it at the expense of our last memory of my brother and our feelings of grief and heartbreak, or mine at least.

My father took down all the information from the police report and the phone number of the hospital so he could make arrangements to have what was left of Jimmy taken to a funeral home in Quincy. If it had been up to my father, we'd have driven to the hospital in Lawrence, Massachusetts and had one of the refrigerated cadaver compartments opened so he could take a good look at Jimmy's corpse. But my mother lost her composure over the issue. That was one time that my father couldn't overrule her, and we went home without stopping at the hospital morgue and without further discussion.

If you think my parents' reaction to the tragedy was screwy, wait until you hear the next part! My mother asked my father how they were going to notify Dorothy and Barbara about Jimmy's death and how they were going to pay for my sisters to come home for the funeral. I was astonished when the two of them began plotting how they could keep the news a secret. Oh, my good God – another secret! I had to make a promise not to say a word about it to either of my sisters, should they call our house during the wake or the funeral. Neither of them did call and my parents didn't call either of them.

The events came and went, and Dorothy wasn't told until she came back from California a few months later. If I thought she was hurt that nobody had told her or invited her to the funeral, that was nothing compared to how Barbara took the news when she got back from Austria not long afterward. I don't think she ever forgave my parents for keeping it a secret because she would have wanted to make the trip to be there for Jimmy's funeral. After all, Jimmy was her only sibling by birth. What caused the wound to be deeper for her was when she learned the Army would have paid for her trip.

The wake was held near our house, on Hancock Street in Wollaston, diagonally across the street from the Supreme Market. My parents were able to enforce their will that the casket be kept open, and I was glad because I wanted to see my brother again even if he was dead. I never asked how the undertaker accomplished it but there was so much pancake make-up smeared on Jimmy's face that I could only guess what had been done. Otherwise, Jimmy looked amazingly lifelike. So much so that I touched one of his hands hoping that everyone had made a mistake and Jimmy was still alive. When I realized how cold and rubbery he felt, I knew that Jimmy Wah-Wah was gone forever, even though I'd dusted-off my rosary beads and prayed myself to sleep at night, hoping that God would resurrect him.

The first time that nobody else was in the viewing room, I reached into the casket and removed the ring from Jimmy's rigid right hand. I'd always admired that silver ring with the large, square red stone that pretended to be a ruby instead of a plastic called vitalium. Jimmy had made it himself when he worked in a laboratory as a dental technician. I've kept it for sixty-eight years in my desk drawer. It's the only thing of his that I've ever had, and whenever I hold it, I cry and pray that his soul is in heaven and someday, somehow, somewhere we'll be pals, like God undoubtedly meant for us to be.

That was when I began to appreciate that my brother, Jimmy Wah-Wah, was my real hero, not Teddy Ballgame. I began to relinquish my admiration for Ted when I thought about the hardships that Jimmy endured in his life, a life in which everything seemed to be against him. Poor Jimmy never seemed to catch a break. He could have been the Murphy for whom Murphy's Law was named. My brother was more visible to me than any baseball player, closer to me physically than anyone else in the world. I would soon enough learn that Barbara and Dorothy felt the same way about Jimmy – he was their hero, also, which was especially true for Barbara.

Chapter Thirty-five

The real hero

To say that Ted Williams of the Boston Red Sox was the greatest hitter in Major League Baseball and that Captain Theodore Samuel Williams of the United States Marines was the best combat wingman in the Korean War is accurate. To say he was my childhood hero is the understatement of all understatements. It was me who named him 'The Hero of Jersey Street' because the front gate of Fenway Park is located on Jersey Street. But, after the tragedy of my brother's death, I began to see life differently and to appreciate how difficult Jimmy Wah-Wah's life had been compared to how favored Teddy Ballgame's life had been.

It was then that my admiration shifted. After appreciating all of the handicaps and hardships that Jimmy endured in his life, I felt greater appreciation for my brother than Ted because I'd come to realize that James A. Murphy, Jr. was the real hero in my life. All that time he'd been there right before my eyes, but it took a crisis to make me realize how much I respected his ability to endure.

Ted had lots of things going for him. Jimmy had lots of things going against him. Yet despite the odds against him, my brother overcame the trials and tribulations he was forced to accept and, frankly, did most of it without many complaints or much help from the people who should have been there for him, including me. Jimmy had been ridiculed from childhood because of his facial deformities and his speech impediment. Ted succeeded because of his exceptional advantages. Jimmy survived in spite of his exceptional disadvantages. All things considered, I was more inspired by Jimmy than Ted and that's the reality of the situation.

God bless you, Jimmy Wah-Wah. I pray that we will meet again, and next time I'll be certain to tell you that you're my real hero because of your resilience, grit and indestructible sense of humor. I never understood what you were forced to endure until you were gone. If only I had known sooner, I might have been a better brother and a better friend instead of acting like a casual observer. But because of you, I developed an attitude that I could overcome anything and did. I witnessed you fighting the good fight against enormous odds, and I committed myself to doing the same although I was facing much lesser odds. If you were able to get beyond criticism, so could I. If you could keep your sense of humor when most people would have been doomed, so could I. Thank you for the example that you provided me. I pray that we will meet again and rejoice in each other's presence and God's love.

Well, there you have it – that's my story and I'm sticking to it. It explains how a 5th grade teacher, a 10-year-old girl, a bus trip to Fenway Park, a field of lime Jell-O grass, a Red Sox baseball game, the charisma of a sports hero and the compassion of a Boston cop changed the life of a confused kid who otherwise might have wound up in the nuthouse. In fact, I'm convinced that's how I avoided being in the nuthouse. Had it not been for Miss DiMascio's 5th grade field trip, Molly Noonan's affectionate grasp, a Red Sox historical victory, an encounter with Teddy Ballgame and a chance meeting with Lou, the Boston cop, who knows where I might be today? The field trip steered my life in a positive direction that appears to now be headed toward the glorious pearly gates of heaven instead of toward the ominous, black gates of hell.

So, parents, take heed: If you have children who can't seem to get their lives together, instead of threatening them with frightening outcomes, send or bring them to a professional sports event or another entertainment event of their choice and let nature take its course. That's how I escaped the condemnation of excommunication, hell, jail and the nuthouse.

If only I had known then what I know now, I'd have kept holding Molly Noonan's hand during the bus ride to Fenway Park, proudly introduced her to my mother and announced to everyone within earshot that I'd fallen in love. I was so deliriously thrilled to be with Molly that I should have asked her to marry me, right then and there. I could have given her my Captain Midnight decoder ring to let the world know that we were engaged. After that, I could have started saving my weekly allowance so that one day we could afford a pair of Red Sox season tickets behind home plate.

We could have settled down somewhere around Quincy and lived the American dream together. We might have had three sons, a four-bedroom house, a convertible, a station wagon, a motorboat, a yacht club membership, a beach house on Cape Cod, a golden retriever named Buddy, not to mention a calico cat named Boomer. But, for whatever reason, all of those things never happened that way.

When I was ten, how could I have known that I was in the presence of some of the greatest inspirations of my lifetime, all on the same day? How would I have known that I'd never experience another day as euphoric as Thursday, June 8, 1950? A fortuneteller with a turban, a crystal ball, a genie in a bottle, a spoonful of tea leaves, a handful of pixie dust and a magic wand couldn't have predicted an outcome that sensational. If only I hadn't been too love-struck to tell Molly that I adored her. If only I hadn't been too star-struck to ask Ted for his autograph.

Unfortunately, after I left Fenway that day, I never saw Ted in person again. Unfortunately, after I left elementary school, I never saw Molly in person again. It was like having been at the top of the world without realizing where I was and that I'd never be there again, even though I was destined to live for at least another seventy-three years and counting.

In spite of my failed romance with Molly and my failed friendship with Ted, looking back, I can recognize just how much the events surrounding that visit to Fenway Park uplifted me. I realize now how firmly that day shaped every future day of my life and how much clearer my outlook became as a result. On that divinely inspired day I learned that life could be more exciting, more joyful and more fulfilling than anyone had ever explained to me, more than I'd ever learned on my own.

From that day forward, my mind's eye was able to see light at the end of life's tunnel, which was a revolutionary change for me; I'd never been able to see anything but gloom, doom and despair before that. If patience is a virtue, I became virtuous waiting for the Red Sox to become world champions which has occurred four times. If persistence breeds success, I became successful because of my indestructible loyalty to the Sox. Everything worthwhile that I've accomplished in life can be traced back to June 8, 1950. I'm convinced that it was then, and not a day sooner that my life took a miraculous upturn for the better.

But it wasn't until I was fifteen that I got a more realistic understanding about what heroism really is. It was the sudden, accidental death of my brother that provided me with a clearer understanding of heroism. Heroism is not confined to talented athletes and courageous patriots. It is best understood in situations where people rise above overwhelming odds against success, become exceptional achievers in spite of the condemnation and ridicule of others and maintain a sense of humor about life no matter what obstacles, hardships and pain they have been forced to endure. It's about being resilient, optimistic and believing in yourself.

Teddy Ballgame? Exceptionally talented athlete and exceptionally courageous patriot. Jimmy Wah-Wah? Exceptionally resilient overcomer and exceptionally brave warrior. Ted was an example of achieving exceptional success by maximizing his superior talents and superior abilities.

Jimmy was an example of bravery and endurance in the face of staggering odds for failure. But Jimmy graduated from failure to success in my eyes, when I was fifteen and I was considering his accomplishments as I looked at his lifeless body in a polished mahogany casket at Dewar's Funeral Home in Wollaston, Massachusetts.

Since then, Jimmy Wah-Wah has been my constant choice as the greatest hero I've ever known and my constant companion as the best friend I always wanted. Hardly a day passes when I do not think about Jimmy and tell him in my mind and heart that I love him.

When Jimmy's casket was lowered into a grave at Mount Wollaston Cemetery, part of me had also died but another part of me was born at the same instant. The gravesite my father purchased was in front of a stone wall that looked like the one I remembered from the time my friends and I watched a burial there for the first time. Maybe God had been preparing me for Jimmy's burial then and maybe the message now was that Jimmy had embarked upon another trip, like his train trip to Massachusetts when I was five, only this time to heaven. He was twenty-seven years old and wouldn't have to fight the good fight any longer. The day of Jimmy's burial had become more inspirational than the day of my field trip to Fenway Park. Not as exciting, of course, but more inspirational, and it has become more meaningful as I've grown older. Jimmy Wah-Wah deserved heaven more than anyone else I've ever known.

When I used to believe my mother's threats about

getting excommunicated, going to jail, going to the nuthouse or going to hell, I had no hope, only fear and discouragement. After the field trip to Fenway, I've been convinced that when people have hope and confidence about the future, the windows of heaven fly open, prayers are answered, dreams come true, and miracles occur.

All you have to do is believe. How hard is that? Jimmy's tragic death made that even clearer to me. I'm proud to admit that I'm still following Jimmy Wah-Wah's example of resilience. I'm still wishing upon a star and still wondering if I'll be going back to that place among the stars where I thought I'd come from when I was a kid. Here are the wishes I'm hoping will come true whenever I pass through those pearly gates:

Please, Lord, let there be baseball in paradise – may the grass look like lime Jell-O and the clouds look like whipped cream once more.

Please, Lord, let me apologize to Molly Noonan for spoiling her field trip – I'll gladly hold her hand again if she'll let me.

Please, Lord, let me give Ida Mae DiMascio a world-class hug for bringing me to a Red Sox game – it was the best thing a teacher ever did for me.

Please, Lord, let me thank my mother for letting me go to Fenway that day – I realize now that her harsh discipline was intended to make me a better person.

Please, Lord, let me thank my father for his silent support of my needs in spite of his need to tolerate most of my mother's behavior.

Please, Lord, let me thank my sports hero, Teddy

Ballgame, for inspiring me with his examples of courage and strength on and off the baseball fields of North America, on and off the airfields of South Korea. How I'd love to see Teddy Ballgame again and watch him hit a baseball again – that was a thing of beauty! Perhaps I'll find the courage to speak to him next time and I have chosen to believe in a next time.

Finally, Lord, let me play catch with my brother Jimmy so that I can tell him that I love him, hug him and apologize for never hugging him before he was killed. I'm so grateful for his examples of courage and strength dealing with the adversities caused by his birth defects and by the lack of respect he endured during his life. How I'd love to be with Jimmy Wah-Wah once more, even if he throws rocks at me again. Jimmy is the real hero about whom I have chosen to believe that I will meet again.

Of all the personal heroes I've ever known, there was never anyone as inspirational as Jimmy Wah-Wah. Of all the sports heroes I've ever seen, there was never anyone as inspirational as Teddy Ballgame. As much as I regret that I never spent enough time with either of them, my fondest wish is to have another chance. I can only dream that I'll find Jimmy and Ted having a catch together in a heavenly outfield when I get there.

Reflecting upon the seventy-three years since the big bang occurred in my life, I have become convinced that Jimmy was more heroic than Ted in terms of the contribution his life and death made to my life. Thank you, God, for allowing Jimmy and me to have shared twelve years living together and for allowing me to

share in the glow of his heroic life since then.
Amen.

Chapter Thirty-six

Where's Molly?

Most people, when they've read the story, have the same initial response: 'That was interesting but where's Molly?' So, I began a search to find the answer. I learned that she had become a registered nurse and migrated to the Midwest. There she had become the director of a nursing program at a large medical complex, a respected consultant on nutritional issues and the author of articles appearing in medical journals. Upon retirement, she returned to Quincy and although I found two possible addresses, I was unable to get a response to my attempted contacts. A year or so later, I searched again and found an address for her in Falmouth, at the southwestern tip of Cape Cod, about 125 miles by car from my home. Although I twice sent her a letter with a synopsis of the story and a return address, I did not receive a response.

Another year passed and, not having a better plan, I decided to drive to the address in Falmouth and walk up to the front door to see what would happen. I was prepared to leave her a letter if nobody answered the door. But the door was opened by a pleasant, perky woman with short, blond hair who introduced herself as Valerie, Molly's granddaughter. She told me that Molly was a paraplegic as the result of numerous strokes, and she preferred not to see visitors. When I mentioned the 5th grade field trip and the bus ride to Fenway Park, Valerie invited me to come in and have a seat so that she could hear more about the book and her grandmother. When I came to the part about holding hands, Valerie broke into tears.

She crossed the room toward me and extended her right hand, motioning me to follow her down the short corridor to a sunny bedroom with a window looking out toward woods and water. The room had lavender wallpaper imprinted with images of blue and green hydrangea bushes which, according to Valerie, were Molly's favorites. I had my first look at Molly since elementary school and instantly recognized the twinkle in her eyes. I was sure that the bedridden lady wearing a quilted, pink robe was Molly, the mature version of my first love.

Although her grandmother seemed to be alarmed by this intruder coming into her room without warning, Valerie walked to the side of the bed, took Molly's right hand and announced that the tall, elderly man with her was someone who had been in love with her for seventy-three years and was there to tell her how important her memory has been to him. I was surprised when Molly began to weep and asked Valerie if I was Bob Murphy. When Valerie acknowledged that I was, Molly wept harder as her chest filled and emptied with deep sighs and labored breathing.

As Molly extended her right hand to me, Valerie

signalled me to go to her. When our hands touched, I leaned down and kissed the back of her petite hand and the most amazing thing happened. Molly whispered to me, 'I loved you too, Bob Murphy and I wanted you to come here ever since you sent me that letter several years ago but I was too embarrassed to let you see what an old, shrivelled bag I've become.'

I answered by telling her that she was the most beautiful bag I'd seen since I was ten years old. As she reached her right hand to my neck, we kissed each other on the cheek. It was the perfect ending to my dream, to the book and to a wonderful, meaningful day. I promised her that I would return whenever she felt up to it. Her last words were, 'You're welcome anytime, even if you were too embarrassed to hold my hand on the bus ride to Fenway Park.' We both smiled, giggled and said a fond adieu.

My drive back to Connecticut had a sense of completion about it, some people would have called it closure. There was a call from Valerie at seven-fifty that evening informing me that Molly had died peacefully several hours after I left and that she had a peaceful smile on her face. Her last words were, 'Tell Bob Murphy I'm going home; maybe he'll visit me there some day.' I was overcome with passion because that was what my mother had said to me three hours before she died twenty-two years earlier.

The following week I attended Molly's burial service in Quincy, at the Mount Wollaston Cemetery where my father, my mother, my brother and my sister, Dorothy, had previously been laid to rest and where I expect to be buried someday. I was able to see the headstone at my family's grave from Molly's grave. 'Close enough,' I thought to myself. Please indulge me by saying a prayer that we will meet again someday in heaven, Molly and me, God willing.

February 14, 2023

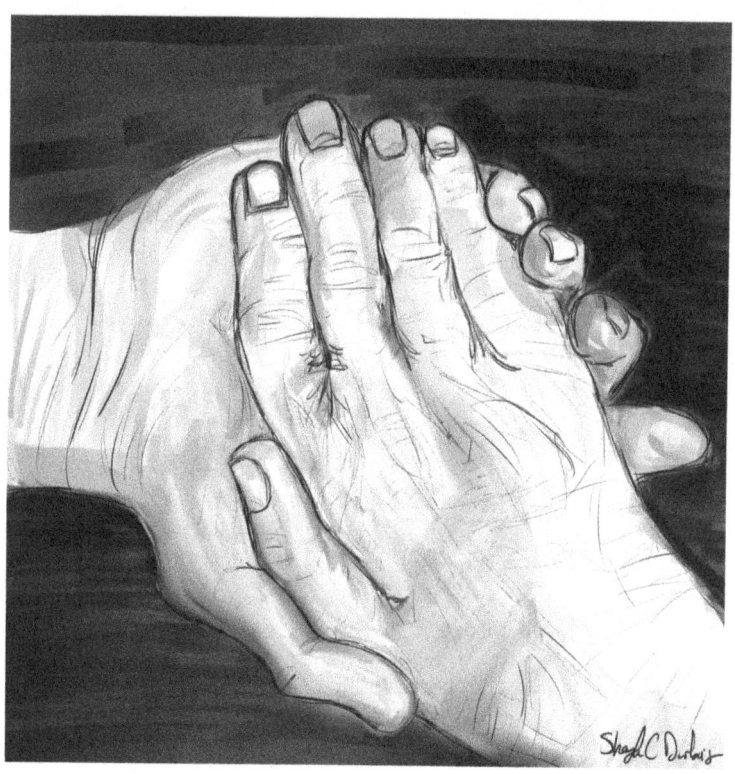